How to Argue

Easy Step-by-step to Win Arguments

(Expand the Boundaries of Your Thinking through Resolving Conflicts Based on Reason and Empathy)

Mark Leathers

Published By **John Kembrey**

Mark Leathers

All Rights Reserved

How to Argue: Easy Step-by-step to Win Arguments (Expand the Boundaries of Your Thinking through Resolving Conflicts Based on Reason and Empathy)

ISBN 978-1-7779885-5-5

No part of this guidebook shall be reproduced in any form without permission in writing from the publisher except in the case of brief quotations embodied in critical articles or reviews.

Legal & Disclaimer

The information contained in this book is not designed to replace or take the place of any form of medicine or professional medical advice. The information in this book has been provided for educational & entertainment purposes only.

The information contained in this book has been compiled from sources deemed reliable, and it is accurate to the best of the Author's knowledge; however, the Author cannot guarantee its accuracy and validity and cannot be held liable for any errors or omissions. Changes are periodically made to this book. You must consult your doctor or get professional medical advice before using any of the suggested remedies, techniques, or information in this book.

Upon using the information contained in this book, you agree to hold harmless the Author from and against any damages, costs, and expenses, including any legal fees potentially resulting from the application of any of the information provided by this guide. This disclaimer applies to any damages or injury caused by the use and application, whether directly or indirectly, of any advice or information presented, whether for breach of contract, tort, negligence, personal injury, criminal intent, or under any other cause of action.

You agree to accept all risks of using the information presented inside this book. You need to consult a professional medical practitioner in order to ensure you are both able and healthy enough to participate in this program.

Table Of Contents

Chapter 1: Research to be Better Prepared 1

Chapter 2: Personalize the Relationship to Win 25

Chapter 3: Minimize Anxiety 39

Chapter 4: Create Value 84

Chapter 5: Understanding Arguments in Relationships 96

Chapter 6: Communication in Relationships 102

Chapter 7: Identifying Your Communication Style 107

Chapter 8: Identifying Your Partner's Communication Style 114

Chapter 9: Understanding Emotional Intelligence 120

Chapter 10: Identifying and Managing Emotions during Arguments 126

Chapter 11: Understanding the Importance 131

Chapter 12: Conflict Resolution Techniques............................ 136

Chapter 13: Managing Power Struggles 140

Chapter 14: Managing Differences in Relationships 145

Chapter 15: Handling Financial Disagreements...................... 151

Chapter 16: Handling Parents' Disagreements Parenting..................... 159

Chapter 17: Dealing with Conflicts over Intimacy 167

Chapter 18: Rebuilding Trust after an Argument............................. 173

Chapter 19: Seeking Professional Help. 178

Chapter 1: Research to be Better Prepared

When we engage in negotiations, we are looking to improve our own circumstances or to avoid some kind or pain. In order to be successful when it comes to negotiations for professional or personal reasons you must be clear about what you want from the negotiation and also the goals you wish to accomplish. We all know what we are looking for. But, what we really want are the things that you must be prepared to fight until the point of death for like shelter, family, the life you live. The things we would like but, if essential, we can do without. Understanding your own threshold for need is vital in setting the parameters of negotiations, along with your strategy and strategies. The most important thing is knowing the needs of your clients helps determine the threshold where you can quit the negotiation table.

In short to reiterate, You as well as Rasp each have their own requirements and desires. Abraham Maslow's 1943 article "A Theory of Human Motivation" in the Psychological Review on need theory provides the motivational forces behind the human mind, inspire us, and determine a large portion of what we conduct. As negotiator crucial is the distinction between what you want and what you need. If you're able to spare a minute, take a look at his books in the field of Need Theory.

In the course of negotiations, note the reaction of Rasp to your proposal or offer. Being attentive to his reaction, you could determine if you're violating the need or desire by observing Rasp's non-verbal response. This will give you an idea of which tactics you should employ next. However, be aware that this can be used in both directions. The way that Rasp reacts tells you a lot about his wants and also the extent to which you're getting towards threatening the basic necessities. Your response to Rasp's proposal will reveal the extent to which you're involved in negotiations and whether you need to cut the conversation. Also, the way you react to Rasp's suggestion could end up giving you information about your needs and requirements, and also indicating whether you are able to bargain.

People don't conceal their feelings well. You should see a clear negative relationship between Rasp's reaction when threating a desire or need. The threat of the need can trigger an extremely strong reaction opposed to the threat of losing of a desire. If you want to know more about ways to improve your effectiveness as a negotiator, think about using Maslow's Need-Theory Model as a situational thermostat.

Being aware of our individual requirements and desires allows us to determine the arguments that warrant an argument and can be dealt with more peacefully in order to maintain a lasting relationship. When we are in the workplace or at home or in a group of friends, we engage in order to convince Rasp to perform our will. We're a species that competes. If we feel it's more important succeed rather than obtaining the items we require then we chance of being offended by Rasp and destroying vital relationships with our spouses close family members, and even our friends. Avoid making the desire winning a routine. It's unattractive, or even detrimental to your relation.

Each Rasp has a ego and emotions that need to be weighed. If you are constantly yelling at your spouse, and insist on compliance during arguments, don't get amazed to find out that Spouse Rasp is withdrawn and might even seek refuge by embracing another person. Spouse Rasp is a powerful player when it comes to negotiations since it is always a possibility of dissociating from the relationship. If Spouse Rasp gets down, it could cost you something important in your life. You must ensure that the issue you're fighting about is worth the mental harm you could cause for the sake of winning. Take into consideration the costs of the issues being discussed. This is the battle you're trying to win, not a battle. Use your strategies to win in essential conflicts. Learn the best way to manage your response to minor conflict.

The use of persuasion to win over affection will help you build the relationships you have with your family and friends. It is possible to lose your friends in the event that you're person who is a bully when you are negotiating with your friends. It is a matter of deciding which movie to see, what eateries to choose, and what kids you will allow to join the group, all of these require negotiation with your peers and potential new friends. What you do together with your Rasp can determine the character of your relationships in the future with them.

Negotiating is a form of social interactions that are required for those who live within a group. If you're not eager to live in a cave, consider Friend Rasp's wants, needs as well as desires and emotions. Consider what you'd like in terms of importance to you, and just how crucial the matter is for the Friend Rasp. Most of the time, you can obtain the things you want without burning your friendship with the person you consider to be Friend Rasp through conciliatory methods.

NEGOTIATING V. BARTERING

Experience usually enhances your abilities to negotiate. Professional negotiators have specializations within that they can exercise. This is expert knowledge within the area of the issue being discussed but not when it comes to negotiations. It's a huge difference.

Negotiation expertise does not depend on ability to master the art of negotiation but rather the ability to master the subject of negotiation. Knowing how to negotiate is essential, however mediators and arbitrators are chosen by courts according to their expertise in the field (construction and real estate the legal profession.). Donald Trump is a skilled business tycoon, and one of his strengths is that he's the most effective negotiator. His business acumen which makes him stand out as a successful business person.

Negotiating is an art. As we all are required to bargain, it's important to understand. There's an incredibly distinct difference between negotiations and bartering. Bartering is the exchange products based on greed and the desire to be greedy. Bartering is the unidirectional trade of a commodity an alternative. In bartering, Rasp seeks to maintain an equal value in exchange for the commodities.

Negotiation on the other hand is a process that involves Rasp seeking to generate value. In order to reach the agreement comes from Rasp seeking an avenue to persuade you to accept some (or all) of his demands. In this instance, Real Estate Rasp needs to be aware of the importance of time, options ownership financing, entitlement concerns markets, conditions of the market, rate of interest, chain of title concerns and every other element involved in the development of land that significantly affect the worth of a piece of land. In understanding the different limitations and possibilities for development to a particular parcel of land, Real Estate Rasp can mitigate the seller's desire for the highest amount of cash in exchange for a higher price than Real Estate Rasp wants to make. The chance Real Estate Rasp is willing to accept to increase the opportunities for development is what creates worth in the deal. Each Real Estate Rasp and seller are satisfied with the outcome.

Learning to assess the diverse currencies that are associated with an event allows you to submit reasonable ideas for Real Estate Rasp or deflate excessively optimistic expectation. Making your case heard, and staying within the The limits that Real Estate Rasp can tolerate it is a skill. This requires knowledge of the subject.

When it comes to negotiations the process of making an offer can be a difficult task due to the uncertainty. To make a convincing proposal one must know the outer parameters of what Rasp will think is reasonable. It is important to note that reasonable isn't the same as what Rasp thinks is acceptable. What you should be able to justify as being an offer that is reasonable to Rasp. You are free to present an offer that is aggressive but be prepared for being confronted by Rasp. Your offer's impact is contingent on how you defend your offer. Untrue offers will expose your character as a fraud and undermine your credibility significantly.

A personal encounter I had in negotiating the lease of a customer I taken comparable rates for leases, vacant rates, and evaluated the dynamism of the micro-market. With a clear knowledge of what leases were in the market above or below and the possibility of a market for spaces, I was at the point of making an offer. One of the last pieces of information I required prior to making my offer was details about the landlord. I wanted to know how well informed the landlord was on the market value of his home. Some landlords are extremely pro-active, while other landlords remain passive.

I had a meeting with the landlord and his wife following a tour of the surrounding area. My goal during the conversation was to learn the most I could about their actual estate portfolio, their plans for investing, and also their understanding of the marketplace and their property. If the moment came to present an offer I did not make it an offer as such. I didn't want to talk about the intrinsic worth of the land. However, I did want to convince people of what the lease was worth the money I proposed. I explained that the lease, if analyzed according to the conditions I planned to offer as well as based on the creditworthiness of my client's, could yield "X" to the landlord, "Y" to their lender and "Z" to a third person buyer. These appraisals broadened the buyer's viewpoint from their perspective of the value in relation to what they might obtain by refinancing or selling their property under the lease. I also added future value potential into the formula.

In observing their satisfaction satisfied with the value I could easily offer less rent to the landlord as I'd added in their view, the extra benefits of an agreement with my client as tenant. If I'd just mentioned that the rent was not included in the preamble to the methods for valuing leases, they may have been sceptical of the low rate of rent and might have kicked my name out as a waste of time.

The end result was that I came to a tad over the rent, but not anywhere near what I would be willing to pay but not even close to the amount they had originally looking for. However the couple was happy by the deal. The property that they were able to sell. This was something I'd learned during my first conversations with the couple. Although their first goal was to get a higher rent, I was able concentrate them on their main purpose of selling. A objective that became increasingly significant for them.

The process of negotiation can be very lengthy. The key is to assess whether the time spent to prepare is worth it or economical. In the end, the advantage of knowing the facts usually allows the person to complete a superior job. In this case, the couple who owned the property needed to be pushed to accept a lower rent than the request price. My goal was to prove how the landlord could benefit from my client being an occupant, though at lower cost. My arguments were founded upon the benefits of a tenant's tenancy, not the rent. The additional time I spent studying the long-term plan of the landlord helped me to help my client save lots of dollars. It was well-invested time. However, not every negotiation is worth the extra effort.

In order to maximize your chances in important negotiations, ensure you are knowledgeable about Rasp prior to trying to talk about specific points. My personal experience has taught me that across a range of scenarios people who have more understanding of the parties involved and their issues are more effective than a lot of professional negotiators. As an example, a number of real estate developers can beat their corporate negotiators due to their knowledge regarding their property. Why? Since corporate negotiators can be too engaged in securing 10-12 sites per year, while the landlord's focus is his own task. Corporate site selection specialists need to spend sufficient time looking over the particular site as well as learning about the landlord so that they can do the most effective job possible for their business, and do not hurry through the negotiation procedure to earn a larger personal benefit based on their productivity.

If there is a third-party negotiation in which one party is making use of a professional or paid attorney, the advocate should be disciplined and concentrate on the requirements of the client, not trying to keep track of time in order for the time to reach the course adding time billable or seeking to maximize any incentive.

I was a mediator for a couple who was just getting married. The couple was considering divorce however their priest suggested mediation before. I was an option last resort. They were well conscious of their own discontents and personal experience. I didn't know anything about their current situation, their hopes or even their targets and plans. What I did know was that they were in pain and needed aid. It was my responsibility to find out about each one of them by themselves, what each would like and require from the mediation. A large part of it was trying to figure out what they were looking for from one another as well as their relationships to determine whether there was a reason to fight to keep it.

In spending time in private with them, I learned about what I was required to be aware of. It was a procedure of going through the complaints they had and determining which was the most important issue and what were the irritants provided the couple a fresh perspective on their issues. I helped the couple understand why they were began their relationship in the first instance and also how their little irritations were out of hand. They ultimately decided to make their relationship work by remaining focussed on the most important aspects. As mediator in this situation, I couldn't be able to negotiate any resolution without spending enough time learning about the couple and their desires and requirements. Negotiating can be difficult. It's not a quick process. It can, however, be in this case extremely profitable!

In negotiating the purchase of homes, what's crucial isn't so much what the cost of purchase, but more importantly the terms of purchase. We all need secured a loan to fund such an purchase. The price and the down payment will determine the amount you borrow, the rate of interest and credit score will determine your amount of payments you make each month. The price can only be acceptable if you are able to afford the monthly payments. The current culture of purchasing credit items that we cannot afford has dragged thousands of us to financial shackles. The over-extension to purchase items which we don't need and aren't able to afford damages businesses and marriages alike. In the present, we're seeing cities such as Detroit and Stockton having to declare bankruptcy. The loans with the lowest initial costs made it easy to enter the market for housing. However, this happy ending became a personal tragedy after rates rose and banks closed.

Investigate before committing. The current employment climate and the conditions of increasing payments are a serious issue. In negotiating for a loan from Lender Rasp, the initial payment is crucial, but be sure that you know the method and time when the payments can increase. Find out the highest amount the loan payments will increase. Consider how much your income will have to rise in order to pay for the loan. This loan repayment is money from your wallet as well as the pockets of your children and spouse. If you are granted one, will be decreased by taxes as well as savings plans, among other charges. You must therefore ensure that the next increase you're anticipating will be a possibility and whether it can cover the increased amount of loan. Next, you must be aware of what could happen should you are fired for 90 days, six months...or more. Many families risk their lives when they sign loan agreements and not understanding all the terms. Lender Rasp is typically paid according to the loans he is able to secure but not on how financially viable the person who is borrowing! Lender Rasp will be selling the loan and has no incentive to assist you in understanding the finer points.

Good negotiators value the importance of getting accurate background information from people around them prior to stepping into discussions with Rasp. However, be aware that advice can be expensive. Most people have opinions or wants to offer suggestions. Similar to how good background information regarding Rasp could be helpful during the negotiation process, advice that is not followed correctly can cause confusion.

Researching background information about Rasp from third-party sources or other parties who are not directly involved in negotiations can help prepare for negotiations. The information should be authentic and vetted. For instance, you shouldn't to ask your aunt Gertrude to give you advice regarding how to deal with the IRS ahead of any audit...unless you know that your aunt Gertrude is actually retired IRS agent, or is a frequent victim of having been subject to audits. It is possible to seek her guidance on how to do something extra special for your spouse that is her most beloved family member.

The information you receive regarding Rasp may be inaccurate or incorrect. Keep in mind that the information you pass through is "filtered" by your source. This means that it is affected by your source's experiences working with Rasp. You must verify the data you collect from other sources by utilizing various sources. If it is found to be accurate and meaningful in your discussions with Rasp and you are able to verify it, then you might be able to trust the information. Be cautious not to fall for misinformation in believing that such tips or details concerning Rasp is true.

In the final step of validation as a final validation step, it's a good procedure to obtain the background details of Rasp through as numerous different sources as you can before making it easy to summarize the information into important impressions. When you actually meet with Rasp make sure to confirm your information by monitoring Rasp's non-verbal and verbal reactions. Often, the information is altered and credible sources may be inaccurate.

As an instance, when I wanted to buy the property, the sources I spoke to told me that the asking price was fixed and offers lower have been turned down previously. The property was on the market for a long time and the seller has always stood firm. In my meeting with the seller, we talked about all things... however, we did not discuss the price. In our conversation, I discovered that the seller also had an possibility that needed cash in order to fund the deal. On the next day, I submitted an offer that was based on my offer that was cheaper than what was being offered. It was an all-cash offer that had a swift closing designed to meet the demands of the seller's another chance. The entire group was amazed at the quick acceptance of the deal.

Before my appointment, I'd gathered very reliable data. It was to be confirmed in the face-to-face discussion. The data I gathered appeared to confirm the firm price guidance I received. However, during meeting's "getting-acquainted" preamble to the discussion, I discovered that some things might be different. It is my usual practice to ask a string of questions open to the public in order to encourage people to talk about their own lives. At these events, the aim isn't to speak however to listen, and then pose follow up questions to gather details in a casual manner.

There are numerous reasons to inquire about the latest data from Rasp. The most crucial factors is finding out what's changed recently and whether the changes have an impact on negotiations in the near future.

Like in the home purchase case, learning about the buyer's requirement for cash as we got to know one another I gained a significant advantage in negotiations. I was fortunate to have money at hand to buy the house. Therefore, I was able make use of that unique time in my favor. I was able buy the house at a price that was lower than market since at that point the cash value was greater for sellers more than price.

In a discussion, granting some power to Rasp by surrendering control could work as a strategy. You may have heard of the tale of a mother who had two brothers fighting over a big slice of cake. They were afraid that if the cake was cut in two parts, the second would receive a bigger portion. In order to stop the anticipation of argument Mother gave the older son a knife and instructed him to slice the cake. The boy was thrilled! However, the mother handed his brother the option of picking his first piece. This aspect of control pleased each of the sons. Each had some sense of control over what happened.

The method has a variety of applications. In the first session of tennis My group has embraced the idea of having one team start first, and another team picks the side. Each has advantages. The first team to serve is the most likely to winning the opening game, and thus starting the set ahead. The second team, deciding which side to play on will be able to determine where they should put themselves in the court, in comparison to winds, sun and other external elements, and gain an advantage in court positioning in the set.

In the end, each team is satisfied in the negotiations as they each have their own share of the decisions which affect the play. When negotiating, in order to be successful, you need confidence that Rasp is going to perform according to the conditions of any deal reached. The best way to guarantee this is when Rasp believes he's achieved something that is at the very least fair out of the deal. In the absence of feeling completely in a rush to make a decision this, the likelihood of Rasp is likely to renege on the arrangement is significantly decreased.

Chapter 2: Personalize the Relationship to Win

Researchers have looked into the methods primates study learning. One study included an extremely young group of Chimpanzees as well as children. The group of chimps and children was provided with the basics of how to open devices. The chimps as well as children were each given their own devices that they could use.

The chimps fought hard to get the devices open. They utilized their prior ability to experiment randomly. The kids were, however used the techniques they'd seen and attempted to unlock the device using the specific method only. They were much more efficient.

It is through our interactions with the other, as well as by studying the behavior of others. These observations are collected and save them for be used in the future for applications. Chimps on the other side, appear to take on every new challenge with enthusiasm but without a lot of application to their previous experiences.

Professions that negotiate as part of their job have been trained to improve their social abilities. They utilize their initial interactions with Rasp to aid in the strategy they employ to negotiate. The insights into Rasp that could prove beneficial in a negotiation are collated and kept to be used in the future. Sometimes in the current fast-paced world, the development of a strategic partnership with Rasp is overlooked to save time and moving on to the next step. This could be an expensive mistake.

In my college days, I wanted to purchase a vehicle quickly and did not see any reason to build a relationship with the vendor. The seller was interested in several buyers and eventually offered the car to an individual who paid less than the price I previously offered.

After the seller had informed me his decision, I inquired as to why he chose to take the lesser amount. His answer was an instruction for me. He told me, "She said she really required it in order to go on with her work. She mentioned that she has an infant to feed. I felt like helping her."

It taught me two important things at an early age: 1)) money is just one factor in any negotiation, and) building a rapport with Rasp is vital.

The transaction was never one of my personal issues, but she was able to create an individual need within the seller's head which trumped my more expensive but less emotional proposal. Human beings are human and humans react to personalization in nearly any circumstance. We are human beings to be social.

Establishing a relationship A RELATIONSHIP OPENING Communication channels ought to be reserved for more crucial situations, don't you think? Wrong! Whether you're at a meeting, on the phone, or conversing/interacting with a sales person over a retail counter there is almost always time to make a friend of Rasp. It is almost always possible to establish a connection with Rasp prior to negotiating.

In negotiating for a quick food customer against a huge experienced, well-trained and tired director of a company for development, I had to contend with a person who seemed to be prone to reject my request based on the fact that my client's intention to make use of the site as a fast food establishment. The only way I was able to get to negotiate with his secretary through a pledge to not exceed five minutes from the president's hectic schedule.

The guard was responsible for the gate. My first task was to convince her to schedule me a time. It took me a couple of months of phone calls as well as making myself available on the phone until I was able to get an appointment. However, the conversation and perseverance made a difference.

A few of the methods I employed to be on her side included:

I noted her name, and would always use it when making calls to her.

I called often, and never got angry with her. Instead, I felt how busy her boss be and I resent to cause trouble.

I identified my problem as a personal matter because the head of my business was leaning on me for help in negotiating with her supervisor. I purposely attempted to make my assistant and myself peer-graded in order to win her trust.

It was clear that I would not be going out until I had the time to meet to her boss.

When I was in the President's Office, I had to grab the president's attention. Given the fact that I knew the time constraints of his agenda, I was only able to get only a couple of minutes of his attention. My client was interested in the restaurant to be located at one of the presidential shopping malls. As a private preference, would not prefer that location as one of the tenants. Furthermore, we were unable to provide the same amount of money in comparison to other options, such as banks, restaurants with larger sizes as well as possibly gas stations, as well as several of the more modern fast-casual restaurants.

We didn't have any influence over the guy who was a mere 40 years younger than him, and I had only just a couple of minutes to present my presentation.

Instead of making the most arduous argument of what I would like him to think about in my suggestion, as he wanted me to make and then I wandered at his desk, admiring the old pictures and asking some questions on a couple of them. I asked him how he came to be to be in business and was listening attentively to his tales about surviving the economic downturn as a young man and then building his present empire completely from beginning to finish.

It turned out that the couple owned one of the most significant privately owned commercial development firms in America. It was a fascinating story and an interesting one. The author was keen to share the story. I enjoyed hearing it. It was my goal to communicate that via mostly non-verbal replies, occasionally a smattering of "Really!?" or "Fascinating!" The man was on the floor and I didn't want to disturb the conversation.

After having listened to the rags-to-rich story before getting to business, I told the tale of the person who was the creator of the idea I represented. The story was similar to a did-it-on-his own tale. The president seemed to like the tale enough to let me continue and, in the final moments told me he was aware about our founder however, he did not realize that his business was a part of the idea I had been representing. They were also friends YPO members. It was a selective small group of young business presidents.

I had surpassed my 5-minute time limit at the point I began to think about the motive behind my visit. I sought his assistance in solving a challenge that was causing us to design the website. Instead of starting by submitting a proposal, or requesting permission to use the site I decided to recommend our company should not move forward with the project until the problem was fixed. I offered to help him develop his experience and know-how in engineering and design.

Unconfronted by the decision of rescinding my suggestion He was interested in trying to figure out how he could fix the issue of layout. I allowed him to decide on the direction. It was quite a while since he'd worked on the simplest of issues, and he was happy to teach an untrained person a few tips. As our usage needed a drive-thru, the issue was justified as it would affect parking, traffic flow as well as aesthetics that are important to both the owner and city.

Short story The architect resolved the layout issue and, as a result was able to see that he was not averse to using the layout as he had thought. We had come the idea of a method to hide the drive-through with the highest berms as well as a large amount of landscaping. He became engrossed in aiding me, and capitalizing upon this and enthusiasm, we came up with a way to come up with acceptable business practices that were mutually beneficial. If it weren't for our having established a relationship as a mentor/mentee, I would not be able to get past my initial idea.

The technique isn't unique or innovative, it's just it is not used enough. It is a technique that Benjamin Franklin referenced in his autobiography.

The case of Franklin was that the merchant was adamantly against him, for reasons Franklin did not understand. A few days later, Franklin entered the shop and, as he was there, he pointed to an item on the shop's shelves. Inquiring about it and asking to borrow it to take it home for a couple of days. The gentleman agreed.

After forming a bond by reading the book and the book's contents, the merchant saw Franklin with a completely different perspective. It could dispel some of the rumors that he heard, that influenced his view.

They became close friendships after this. Franklin's approach demonstrates the importance in being able to allow Rasp to be a part of your life instead of trying to force him to accept something and then be dismissed.

The brief period of introduction to build a rapport is a great idea for many different purposes. Clerks at the store can get motivated to do slightly more accommodating by simply giving them an inviting smile and asking them how their day has been. This small effort will result in a positive outcome when you request for them to look into the details of something or to process an amount of money. Making more than a cursory relation between your transaction and the Clerk Rasp is sure to distinguish you from other people waiting on the other side of the counter. If you're in need of assistance then you'll likely receive the assistance you need.

I purchase my food at the local market that is upscale. I have a particular product that both my wife and me love. To ensure that we have it always available, I buy an occasional case and then keep it frozen. It is a custom order and I must call or stop by the store for me to set it up.

I was doing this for a while. Each time, I would strike up conversations with the manager of the Deli or the person behind the counter. We discussed anything I could come up with for a way to distract myself. The only thing I was doing was ensuring they completed my purchase. The company never recorded it or did not take my details, and I was worried that I could get lost in the process of handling the other clients.

A few days later, I came in for my order and was greeted by the manager who said "Hi Bill. Are you here to take your order?" I said I had been there even though I wasn't in fact there to make the order. He responded, "No worries. We've got an extra case exclusively for those who need it. We will be there to help you."

Their extra effort on their part is a benefit of me taking the time to meet them.

In the absence of the power of eternity, you'll require the assistance of other people, a.k.a. Rasp. Spending the time familiar with Rasp typically pays exponential dividends.

The foundation of a partnership on that you can negotiate is demonstrated by the way people are able to approach wedding. There is going to be conflicts. This is the norm. The courtship process, which is a prelude to wedding, is in which two couples form an intimate relationship which, if properly and carefully is able to endure the stresses of two persons sharing a home for an extended duration of time, the marriage. In light of this, when knowing more about Potential Spouse Rasp and the potential for a marriage, it's interesting to ask if the recent trend of shortened courtship time periods in the latter half of the 20th century was a factor in the rising divorce rates.

The constant conflict throughout any personal or marital relationship. One way to maintain the bond is to acknowledge the fact that both you as well as Spouse Rasp are part of an Common Dream: growing old with your grandkids, watching them playing, or exploring through the seven seas in retiring. It's beneficial having a common idea to rely on as you try to put your conflict in the proper context. Do you think yelling at the person who damaged the car worth risking the Common Dream? Most likely not, so take an eagle's grip and get your temper a little. It is possible to apply this technique with any family with a shared goal, such as your spouse, child and parents or friends. It is a way to keep the everyday issues within the context of.

Strong relationships are built on good communication and mutual respect. One benefit of having a healthy connection is that it shares the same dream. A Common Dream concept will be discussed more in depth later.

Chapter 3: Minimize Anxiety

Anxiety can hinder the ability to communicate clearly and effectively. People become defensive, nervous and blocks the chances to you as well as Rasp in achieving a conclusion. If you don't have a massive advantage over Rasp it is advisable to consider a second thought before utilizing the fear of being a threat to manage the circumstance. There are instances that using brute force may be appropriate. When Petty Thief Rasp hides in an alleyway and he appears and threatens you or your spouse as the two of you walk back home from the restaurant you love and he uses terror to force you into acceptance. When faced with this scenario, find a solution that will overpower the threat of fear that has been imposed on your night. If you're capable of bringing in more power, in the shape of the Colt 45, then don't be afraid to take on Rasp's threats by imposing your own. If not, give him your money, thus fulfilling his demands while protecting your own needs a.k.a. your lives. Most of the time, aside from these extreme circumstances it is generally a good idea to lessen and, when you can, eradicate fear or anxiety as often as you can to facilitate interactions via Rasp and find solutions that work for.

When you use fear to get your point across similar to the ones previously mentioned, it must be the intention to sever small Thief Rasp to complete subjection. If you decide to use this strategy in a relationship with family, friends, or your peers, there is a chance that you won't like the impact it has on your relationship. If you are adamant about the connection but you are concerned about the consequences, be aware that it may be in danger if Rasp has the chance to get out of the way. The situation may not be as important if you're dealing with a minor criminal you'd like to never see again, but if there is a person you feel strongly about or deal with, threatening these relationships through your control over them might come at a an enormous personal expense.

Most of the time in business or family situations, no single person is in absolute control over another. This may appear to be the case in the event that one decides to rely on each other, or even risk the relationships to defend themselves such as the abuse of a spouse. However, there are often difficult alternatives to weigh the strength. If you value a relationship, be cautious about applying absolute power without risking the trust relationship. The normal emotional response to fear can effectively block the communication needed to figure to resolve a personal issue or disagreement with a loved one as well as a peer or friend.

Social anxiety caused by emotional stress situations can have a negative impact on communication. The boy, who's unwilling to invite to dance with the girl across the space to dance is seen as to be shy. It is actually than the fear of being rejected by the girl in the dancing floor or perhaps the ridicule of the other students that prevent his from taking the first step. The anxiety is difficult to identify, yet they can make it difficult to communicate clearly and concisely. When negotiating, such fears about the social aspect stand in path of negotiating a solution.

FEAR IS A SOURCE OF POWER

The use of fear is by terrorists to defeat large, well-organized, strong foes. It's as well what strong forces, such as oppressive governments use to sway their own citizens. It is used in order to intimidate people to abandon the need to fight. Negotiating, when faced with this kind of situation is not a viable choice.

In Chicago times, in the past there was a time when a mafia underling used to go into a local bar, and openly inform the owner of the bar that it might be in the midst of an fire. The underling would continue with his story, claiming that a fire could be quite a tragedy. A casual owner could have responded, "No way, we are very careful." After a week, when the bar had a minor fire broke out inside the bar the bar's owner would come back and say that the fire could have been prevented with tiny amount of insurance. The proprietor would be able to learn two important things: 1)) Failure to pay the bill made the risk much greater and) In Chicago the family was the one that was more to be fear than authorities in the area.

The tactic of intimidation forced a lot of law-abiding citizens to purchase security from the mafia in order in order to prevent larger and more destructive accidents or fires. It was not a common practice after the fear had been created. The power of negotiation is a powerful strategy, but it must be employed carefully.

Even though it's 21st century, and we think we live in a modern, civilized society,

Muslim extremists have found that their method of power negotiation, known as terror, creates fear among the more civilized population and promotes their cause. Today, with militaries with heavy weapons that they are aware that they are unable to confront their adversaries' army power on their own, which is why they have to turn to terror acts that target civilians. Random attacks on civilians is intended to create terror.

The best way to protect yourself from powerful negotiators is to not surrender to their fear tactics. Be prepared to take on Powerful Rasp the way you would against a victim. However, some cautiousness in the shape of extra vigilante is necessary to allow you to thwart the strategies used by Powerful Rasp.

A strong sense of purpose and a commitment to the cause you are fighting for could be sufficient. However, anxiety or fear during negotiations is better managed through being well-prepared, educated and confident in the goal you are pursuing. The key to your strength lies in the ability to counter the tricks that are employed by Powerful Rasp. The best way to accomplish this is by anticipating the actions Powerful Rasp might accomplish, or to request the things they want, or even to ask for.

UNDERSTANDING, SOURCING AND USING FEAR

When negotiating, small anxiety that is not related to power, and sometimes connected to relationships or other social factors could play a significant and strategic part in determining the result. The fear of failing, the anxiety of being in the dark and fear about not helping are just a few examples of anxiety that you can use to push your agenda. Profiting from Rasp's fears could also serve in order to counter or diminish his arguments.

One of the strongest strategies that many don't be aware of is the worry from Rasp that she may not seem to assist. Most people want to believe they're concerned for others. everyone wants to be respected and liked. This is the silent motivation that can force Rasp as well as you to perform an act that's inconvenient or inappropriate. This is because the worry that others might think you're not doing the right thing will force you to help others. In this case, for instance, if two people are planning to see different films there is a good chance that at least one is willing to compromise and accept the other's preference and not just because they wish to watch the film however, it's crucial to be loved more than seeing their personal preference. Another, should they'd used the 'if you were truly my friend' ...'card and acted like a friend, could use the friendship to achieve their goals to avoid getting a negative impression of being the true friend. Negotiating techniques are employed throughout our daily situation if we are looking for these tactics.

Sociopaths have no respect to the opinions of other people. He doesn't connect with other people. Most everyone else does. In a business setting most people attempt to remain calm when dealing with a person. We have the lender who states there is no power to assist and the boss who says to you that no pay raises are planned this year due to firm policy, and then the doctor who directs you to the office manager if you ask questions about an accusation. These people can get away with the allegedly sociopathic way of thinking when you don't try to build your own private "bridge" before commencing to examine the important concerns. There are methods to overcome the shield of protection they seek to construct within their own.

Friends strive to keep the relationship, but they are anxious if there is a threat to their relationship. Therefore, it is sensible that you take time to develop a strong personal connection with the people with whom you have to interact prior on with the job at hand. Today, in a fast-paced environment it is not enough time spending time getting acquainted with the individual and then trying to discover the common ground. This means that many chances are missed due to people who are anxious, too fast and apathetic about the benefits gained by establishing connections. And even in our private lives there is evidence of that we must build solid bonds. Today we live in a time that has a very high rate of divorce. Perhaps a little longer courtship may have helped couples who have had failed marriages to develop a more solid marriage that stood against the tests of the passage of time.

What is the most excellent customer service in a shop? The customer who is not rude, however, but those who reach out to greet the clerk with the smile of a kind word or comment. This is the one who the clerk is able to relate with whom the salesperson or salesperson might be inclined to provide a bit of more support. Why? It's not because they need to, however, they do it because they would like to. This is an example of the art of making use of the tactic that makes the worker worried about appearing to assist. If you reach out to them first, with a smile or a kind comment, you've signaled your friendship. You can later let them not bother you further and ring to make a sale, or even return the favor. The majority of us do not like to be viewed as too naive or insensitive, therefore we react in a similar way.

When, as a consumer and a customer, you take the time to create a personal connection however small it may be, you could be able to make Rasp more thoughtful or accommodating. They'll be careful not to offend them. If you can manage the emotions of Rasp you will be rewarded with greater than normal service at the expense of a small smile or gesture of kindness. The outcome of a simple bargain.

Some other examples of common anxieties during everyday negotiation include:

The Fear of Offending

The Fear of Rejection

The Fear of the Unknown

The Fear of Embarrassment

The Fear of Making the Wrong Decision or No Decision

The Fear of Failure

Afraid of Being Offended As we've discussed before, a lot of people worry about offending people, and even strangers. In the present, it's not legally acceptable to speak of anything to everyone in every possible scenario. The majority of people would like to appear as if they are sensitive to other people. Simply put that, they don't intend to look insensitive towards anybody!

In the past, the landlord called me. After hearing that the client was "company X" the landlord sarcastically stated that he wasn't interested in what I said. He did however, not abruptly leave the call. He didn't want to seem completely uninvolved or hostile.

I quickly resigned myself to his decision and stated that I really wanted to hear what he could be saying regarding my client. I then threw him a punch when I said that a part of my job was to get information or input from my client, and to relay critical concerns to the senior management.

It was his opportunity to make himself recognized. I was not prepared for the first reaction he would have given, therefore I turned the conversation around and calculated my reaction to ensure he was talking to me. I used the strategy to capitalize on the initial fear that he had of appearing unfriendly or rude towards me.

When he had the chance to speak and vent, he shared his perspective on the operations. As he elaborated on his situation as well as the more detail I received from him about the things that mattered for the client. As he continued to talk, the more he became involved in the discussion. In a bid to capitalize on his first fear of appearing insensitive I was able to bring the conversation along and to make him at a minimum, comfortable in the conversation. Acceptance by the client was to come after.

We ultimately reached an agreement which was acceptable to both sides. Here is a brief summary of the discussions that removed negotiations

My voice: "Hello, John, I'd like to take a minute to discuss Company X's lease." Landlord: "Good morning Bill. I took your phone call to help you save time and prevent your number from being redialed. It is my understanding that we do not have anything to discuss regarding Company X. I would like to see them leave immediately."

Me: "Really? They must have affected you in some manner."

John: "You could say you could say that. There is no desire to be tenants."

Myself: "I know they have an excellent balance sheet, so there must be something wrong with the way they operate. As I am in an immediate line to the chain, would you be willing to allow me to share with them what's on your mind?"

John: "It won't do much good (pause) But the local management does not really seem to notice. The restaurant is filthy and the operations at unit level are not up to scratch, and it is embarrassing to have guests there, since I'm the owner and this operation is reflecting on me."

Myself: "That's really unfortunate. Both of us know that the site is among their top places. This is a shame that you are unable to connect with your local staff. Let me tell you I'm asking you to give me 72 hours and I'll see what I could do for you to make sure that attention is paid to this issue."

John: "I don't know what good that would do but go ahead, give it your best shot."

Then I went to the client's team and informed them of the situation. The president sent a private note addressed to the landlord, thanking him for his candid remarks and saying he'd take a personal look at the situation. The COO further informed me that I had the option of submitting some suggestions that the company could change its managers at the building and then put in the more knowledgeable managers on the premises when it opens. The two events prompted the landlord to reconsider their commitment to his tenant and sign on reasonable extension conditions in conjunction with me.

It was easy to be scared at the sight of my landlord on the phone in an aggressive way to intimidate me. Instead, I countered the landlord's attack in order to lure the landlord into a conversation, so I'd at least have an opportunity to determine the possibility to establish a business relationship.

Like I mentioned in the final chapter, negotiation is similar to simple broken-field running in football. It is important to be aware of difficulties and then work around the obstacles. Also, you must manage problems when they occur in order to keep your momentum. If you simply go for it straight on will not gain much ground but will result in lots of bruises.Fear of rejection Many people do not want to be disregarded. In many cases, it's evident early in their lives. It is a reason that makes a majority of boys hesitate before asking the most attractive girl at school to go out on dates. The majority of students hesitate before making a gesture to ask an inquiry during the class. If they don't answer correctly it could lead to the disapproval of their teacher as well as the disapproval of their peers. However, if the answer is correct, they may be the target of resentment from the same group of classmates. Rejection is a major fear when it comes to business and social interactions also. Nobody wants to be the one who is last in teams that are chosen. If there's a chance to choose an of work assignment We want to be part of the team. Being unable to be selected, according to us, speaks badly on us and our skills or popularity. We fear being disregarded by people who we'd like to include.

The fear of rejection manifests through a variety of ways. There is also a tendency to accept another. She is busy when her teacher asks her to go out however she is hesitant to inform him that she'll not "not be busy" concerned she may harm his feelings by not liking him. She gives him enough faith that he will continue to seek her. If he isn't angry and abandon the pursuit He will think things through and develop innovative strategies for catching her attention. As time passes and she matures, she will begin to recognize the tenacity of his character, among other traits. In addition, the reason she is reluctant to reject him completely could be due to her fear that the star football player won't invite her to go to prom. And she will not be able to meet a partner.

The practice of dragging participants along is an atypical method of negotiation when the other party wants to sell the product they're offering. In the pursuit of the most affordable price, they do not want to be a victim of a missed possibility. Therefore, they might attempt to keep multiple participants interested, while seeking most favorable price and terms.

If you're at the wrong side of this tactic, evaluate the situation with care. If you decide that there's no possibility of finding a solution Don't spend your time waiting for circumstances to shift. Make sure you are ready to cut right straight to the chase. Create your most compelling offer, however, you must set a date. If it is rejected, you can move on to new chances. There is no guarantee that you will win every opportunity and the time you spend is important. Be careful with your time.

A fear of rejection may prevent people from trying to resolve a issue or to pursue a goal you've always wanted. All of us make assumption. Although many assumption are based on reliable evidence and meet our requirements well, many do not. Others originate from prejudices. Certain assumptions are based upon our fears, or misinformation. Don't let the fear of being disqualified stop your from doing some thing. If you do not ask, you'll not know whether the situation of Rasp is different and you might now be able to convince him of the terms you have set.

Insidious assumptions can hinder efficient communication. Each of us filters the data based upon our individual experiences, beliefs and beliefs. When we color the information and altering it, we modify the input. Make it a routine habit to test or validate your own beliefs before committing to these assumptions. They could turn out to be irrelevant or even completely not true.

A lot of dealmakers in the business do not make aggressive proposals as they fear they'll be ridiculed and disapproved of. I've made offers that are under my customers expectation because I've come up with a way to present an aggressive proposal without causing offence and allowing me to retract the offer before it causes damage.

The method is based on being prepared adequately and establishing an alliance with Rasp prior to proposing a bold proposition, one that's strategically within the realm of being reasonable. It is not and made with a hint of comedy. It is evident the possibility that I could or might actually be serious. This is a way to break the ice. While Rasp doesn't consider my proposition to be real idea, it is often used to elicit a fair response. I have the advantage of asking for the first real request from Rasp without fear of being rejected because of my indiscreetness.

The advantages of this strategy is that sometimes my proposition is less than my client had expected to be able to. So, we're beginning discussions below the amount I was allowed to accept. Now I'm able to focus on the other aspects to enhance the bargain and use price concessions to create leverage. In other words, I'll 'fight to match Rasp's offer through a variety of ancillary concessions as is possible, time being fully ready to give the price that he has already set.

Afraid of the Unknown you answer a knock the sound of a doorbell, nobody would like to walk through a door and not know who, or what's in the opposite direction. Uncertainty is the reason we are hesitant to act on our own initiative or to call to modify a debt to seek financing you need, or ask for the opportunity to be promoted or raised.

The fear of the unknown could include persons you need to work with (your Rashes) as well as the topic issues or just being in a different workplace or location. There is a risk of anxiety when visiting a different physician, switching job or school as well as getting to know a new neighbour. Everything can create fear for being in a new place, particularly situations where you anticipate conflicts.

There is a normal tendency to be nervous when you begin negotiations for the first time. You must realize the fact that Rasp may be the same as you. Beware of letting the facade of an expert deceive you on the reality of this. The first meetings can be a bit intimidating due to uncertainty. Profit from this discomfort by taking action to ensure everyone is at ease in the new environment. If you take the initiative to reduce tensions and begin building relationships that are productive, you are playing a significant leadership role. The confidence shown by this approach can often inspire other people to follow you and turn to you for answers. When you're in a team this could be a very effective negotiation technique.

It is possible to put others at ease, even if you're at someone else's home or office.

Once I was taken into the large, grandiose office of a large developer reputed for being a tough, resolute, "my-way-or-the-highway" landlord. The landlord was not well-known for his penchant to negotiate. As I entered he stood up from his massive table to shake my hand before settling back in his leather-upholstered chair. I was told to sit in the wooden, more humble chair that was across away from the desk.

It was not a coincidence. The design of the furniture was meant to set the power scale against me. Instead of taking the most obvious place, I suggested that we'd prefer sitting at his table in the middle of the space. With aplomb, I made several steps to that end, extending my hand to signal an offer to him to sit with me. (Note that a confident, strong body language always sends a powerful subliminal message for Rasp.) There were two choices for him either be rude or stay behind his desk or go with me. He didn't want to offend me (possibly due to fears of being rejected?) which is why he went to his workstation. We were now both at ease. And, more importantly was that we were set up in a similar way on the coffee table, in chairs.

After a few hours, we come up with a feasible solution. When I entered the room, I found myself in the dark. Once I was there I found a set-up intended to place me in the position of defensive. I spotted the power play, and responded to the power play. As a result, I might create the environment that resulted in my winning when others not succeeded. The reason I didn't do it was in order to make my landlord feel uncomfortable. It was done to create an understanding between us, and foremost in order to inform him that I did not intend to be scared.

In your own way, the anxiety that is triggered by uncertainty can hinder you from trying to accomplish what you're thinking about. Without trying, you'll not know the results you will accomplish. Instead of trying to predict the result beforehand, try taking the chance. Do not try to apply the same strategies and tactics for every scenario. Negative negotiating does not mean you are the way to go about negotiating. Rasp discovers the tactics of your opponent and counters these tactics with ease. Negotiating does not mean performing the same strategy repeatedly. It's not creative and will certainly yield decreasing returns with time. Negotiating is an art form and it is a form of art that can never be predicted. Take advantage of the unpredictability as an opportunity to explore and explore new ways in order to maximize your potential. It's only a matter of time the possibility of making several errors along the way.

The fear of embarrassment is a common one. Nobody likes being humiliated. It is true for plumbers as well as CEOs too. There's a innate fear of their actions if they are unacceptable moral, ethical or even downright unethical actions, they may be exposed to those they cherish - families, friends and even their peers. Nobody wants their poor conduct to be reported to the public!

Sometimes, you may encounter an utterly unethical Rasp. However, you should be cautious not to go over the edge into the realm of libel (which is a crime that could come back to bring you back in a significant manner) Threatening to reveal untruthful behavior of Rasp can be a significant power game and, if have the right information, is likely to result in pressure being placed on Rasp. Since some individuals aren't aware of the law regarding libel, it is recommended to consult experts in the field before you press on the subject to ensure that you are not opening yourself to legal action, whether civil or criminal.

You must be standing on solid ground in order for a credible risk and remain committed to pursuing the plan when confronted. If you're not, this could be a strong force on your behalf.

For a good example the situation, I had to deal with the vice-president of an enormous company that did not want to take what I considered as an appropriate and fair resolution. If he refused the offer, I was able to assume that he was experiencing an issue with our offer because of a motive that was completely unrelated to the transaction. The perception of his reputation was that he could be more approachable if the deal to have something specifically for him personally. My client and me would be involved in these transactions. I decided that it was now time to raise the issue.

I reaffirmed to him the amount the company could be losing if I left. The amount of loss, which could be quantified, was in excess of $1,000,000.00. I inquired if he would really want to turn down the deal outright suggesting, perhaps not in a subtle way that I'd make sure that the top management was aware of the issue.

I had put off doing this till I knew that I had nothing to lose. I was without options in terms of negotiation. Now, he was facing the dilemma of whether I could gain accession to the boss, and in the event that I could, should you actually be able to do so. I effectively communicated my not-so-veiled threat to him in anger, in order to demonstrate my commitment to getting this to a higher degree.

My trick was successful. Fear of being professionalally embarrassed, or being required to justify his behavior to his superiors or even the executive committee pushed him back to the table in an attempt to find a solution. In the end, it was an extremely beneficial bargain for his business as well as mine.

Sometimes you must hit someone over the head to force Rasp follow through with what's right.

The fear of making the wrong decision or any other kind of fear is particularly challenging when two individuals attempt to iron an issue. Inability for both of you Rasp to make a move that will bring the process forward or keep it in a timely manner can hinder negotiations. There are several options to deal with this:

When trying to negotiate in an Rasp stuck in a bind and indecision, make your propositions the form of "either/or" decisions. Instead of forcing a "yes" or no, you can ask the person which option they'd prefer. Do not include the option of 'no.

This strategy can be used as a way for opening up or expanding the dialog. When you ask Rasp to pick among a variety of choices by subtly eliminating the possibility for him to say that no. It anticipates an answer that is positive. The approach lets you present your ideas in a manner which requires Rasp to think about which options is the most appropriate, and which ones seem reasonable. This is more stimulating as opposed to a straightforward either or. It is common to add an additional alternative that is basically an empty slate to allow Rasp to state his own terms. The aim is to stop any rejections and initiate dialogue or any kind of dialog.

If you suspect that Rasp struggles to make important decisions, you can start by making small, minor actions to help make Rasp at ease with the process.

A well-thought out choice should begin with simple, small problems before moving on to larger and more significant ones. It is more appealing psychologically for those worried about making mistakes. The method of decision-tree also makes Rasp used to smaller decisions prior to it is time to tackle the bigger major problems.

A good example of this method for a particular situation is the way a man will prepare to ask his partner for his hand in the marriage. If, in the course of their meeting, he finds out that the person he is interested in has difficulty taking simple decisions like which movie to watch or what dish to order dinner for them, it is best to prepare his partner thoroughly prior to posing the big request.

An ideal approach is to have the person you are interested in early in the process of discussing issues related to their future like where they'd prefer to reside, the kind of house, and how many kids they'd like. The seemingly simple matters and their associated decisions can help to prepare the most important question to be asked by getting Rasp at ease with the thought of having a family together in the future as well as sharing decisions about what the future might look like. And when the main issue is asked, the response will be less difficult, allowing the couple to relax and enjoy this moment. If you still feel anxious or resistance, it could indicate that she's not ready to ask the question, and could not ever be. This could spare your a great deal of stress. There is a chance that you will win.

If you are confronted by someone who is unwilling to make a choice discuss your previous experiences as well as the reasons you took certain actions as well as the benefits of your decisions. Share your personal hesitation to take an unwise choice when faced with a dilemma and explain how it impacted you to come back later. Empathy is a method of calming some worries.

A strategy that has proven successful very well is to utilize an approach of beginning conversations by saying "Bob/Mary I'll be completely understanding that you'll conclude there's nothing you can take action to help." ..." after hearing about your concerns or issues, Rasp may be compelled to prove that initial assertion incorrect and will do everything to show that they are able to help. In asking if they are of any value to you, you have stoked their fears of being seen as unresponsive or unwilling to assist you. They now are determined to prove you that you are wrong, and they have turned into an unintentionally friend.

Take the initiative from people who aren't willing to take a choice.

If you are dealing with middle or lower management Rasp that won't do anything or says there's nothing they is able to do, call the supervisor of Rasp. You shouldn't be complaining about it to Rasp however, you should take your concerns to someone with the authority to aid you. Do not dwell on the fact that the person you're talking to isn't paid to make the decisions. Rasp does not realize how weak she seems and there's no need to turn her into a foe through shaming her. You might need her help later on in the future.

The large bureaucracies or companies often seem to put those in your path that have been trained to tell you, "There is nothing I can do to assist. Really, truly sorry." The reason for this is in order to determine whether the person who inquires won't quit.

In one instance, as I tried to solve an estate problem through a major insurance company I was repeatedly greeted by people who seemed friendly, extremely concerned and willing to assist however, they were of nothing! The majority of them said they had no power and I was unable to communicate with any other person from the department who could assist me.

I had to go through to go through four levels of supervisors, as well as nearly two months of constant phone calls and referrals in order to be referred to a person who actually held control over the department. After I had gotten through the maze, I was successful in gaining satisfaction. The maze was designed there to deter ordinary people and cause delays or omit paying.

If you work for large organizations, you are often having to deal with younger and more inexperienced employees. If you feel they're scared of your position or age, experience or even your title, make sure you ensure you make them feel at ease with your company. Use stories to make people to feel comfortable with your persona and professionalism. Try not to impress them by winning. Your goal is to make the people at ease so that they can open productive negotiations to achieve your goals. In addition, they may relish the chance to fly the flag on the flagpole, or fix the issue. It could even aid in helping to accelerate their career.

Fear of Failure A lot of people avoid taking action due to fear of be a failure. Ironically, the inaction of these people often leads to their failure that they're worried about! In the highly competitive and crowded personnel market, fear of failing in the workplace is more prevalent than it has ever been. Recognizing that Rasp is concerned about this is a way to win essential concessions in negotiations. If you realize that Rasp is under pressure to agree on a solution or resolve the issue then you are aware you've got influence and you are in the in a position of power.

When it comes to credit negotiation, people seeking relief generally desperate to get relief. This is why she'll often agree to unsustainable conditions to buy small amount of time. However, the negative effect of a failure to negotiate to negotiate the right terms can lead to acceptance of terms that usually will just push the debtor and deeper in debt as a result she is unable to come up with acceptable terms.

If you're the borrower You must determine the pressures Lender Rasp may be facing that could provide you with power or influence in negotiation. This could provide you with a leverage when dealing against Lender Rasp. You should not consider

Lender Rasp as the institution which he represents. Lender Rasp is an individual also. Find out how crucial finding resolution for Lender Rasp in order to create some leverage.

If you're working with the collection agent of Lender Rasp look into whether you can exploit the agent's secrets. In particular, the amount he earns might be tied to amount of deals completed, and not the money he collects. If this is the case, does Agent Rasp in line with his quota or will be a performance review that is coming up? Perhaps you can turn it into a position of power through a deal quickly. Avarice among employees is an effective motivation that is often ignored when dealing with the employees of big organizations or institutions, or the state. Be aware that your agreement could directly, personally effect on Agent Rasp might be a source of leverage, particularly in the event that you fail to negotiate the deal has an adverse impact.

The process of sourcing this data is most effective when you're first meeting with a non-threatening, casual way. Try to discover your personal pressure points within the scenario that could motivate Lender Rasp to work with you or things that are causing delays during negotiations. Keep in mind that the lender's stress points could have nothing or no connection to the financial aspect of your circumstance. Be flexible in your approach. A good example of this dialog might include:

Hey I'm a client of yours, and I believe I'm in need of help (soft and non-threatening manner).

Lender Rasp: Good morning. What can I do to aid you this morning?

You: I don't exactly know if you're the one who can assist me. What I'm seeking is some information about the business. What is for instance what is the way that loans are handled? Do they originate here and are managed by corporate, or maybe, even are they sold off?

Lender Rasp: Wow, you don't often get such questions. (You are arousing his curiosity.) Let me know. It all depends on the magnitude that the lender is willing to make. Larger ones, like loans over $XXX XXX.XX can be packaged up and offered by corporations. We keep the smaller ones on our books and control since they're usually our clients and are an intimate relation. (Now you've got yourself a place as long as it's a modest amount of debt.)

You: No kidding. It feels good. The managing team have some vested interests in these loans that are smaller is that right?

Lender Rasp: I know that I have. I personally enjoy such loans as it assists me in helping my friends and neighbors. This bank is a great example of that.

You: Really? What is the reason? Does one get an extra bonus to make loans that are good or being penalized for poor ones?

Lender Rasp: No, no. This is not the same as. The bank is recognized by the top executives for when we prove that we have served the local market with a particular manner. The bank uses these stories in the corporate level to help promote or market the bank. It is likely that the executives receive bonuses, but us worker-bees receive a pat for the job.

Aren't you surprised that this is the norm? Big cheese houses everything they can and demand workers to be hard at work. That doesn't make sense. (You make an ally.)

Lender Rasp: I agree. We are slapped with a hammer when we make them look embarrassed. This could end up costing us our job. It's impossible to predict when it is going to occur. It's my dream to leave here and start my own company. We'll talk about your current situation. ....

It's been interesting to learn a variety of things. The most important one is the fact that Lender Rasp is not secure within his position, causing embarrassment to his bank can cause him to lose his job and is planning for a way to quit and create an enterprise. If you were in this position, consider taking a couple of minutes to ask about the type of company you are working for and whether that you can aid. It was also clear that banks care for its reputation. This is crucial when you're placed in a position to influence the image of the bank positive or negative. You also learned that the loan will be located locally and the decision-makers are likely to be here. You also learned that you could require one or two levels in order to become an executive who has decision-making power in the event that you don't achieve the desired result locally.

If a marital situation is one where there is a person who is more committed to making a marriage successful in comparison to the other one who is committed may feel that she's in a circumstance wherein she has to make concessions to preserve the marriage. One spouse might be feeling the pressure from friends and family members to keep the couple together, and is worried that they'll feel like she's failed when it comes to ending. The lack of trust in the marriage makes spouses who want to quit the lead. The most healthy couples are ones where each spouse has a solid and shared determination to see things through. If not, neither will enjoy the benefit of being able to walk away.

When you realize that Rasp is being pressured by reasons to make an agreement over a certain aspect, you are able to tailor your ideas to gain the maximum impact. Make reference to other, related concerns and propose to resolve these issues to entice Rasp into agreeing to the deal.

I dealt with a challenging issue for a customer and was able to bring the situation to that I believed they were in a great position. The client was stuck on one key aspect and would not compromise further. It's the golden rule The person who owns the gold sets the rules.

In lieu of accepting defeat I decided to return to the table for negotiations, seeking various concessions. I managed to negotiate the concessions on behalf of my client. I returned to him, and reiterated the concessions that I'd secured for him, to determine what if he'd like to consider revisiting the issue that was the most difficult.

Chapter 4: Create Value

Except in physical conflicts, losing does not mean that you lose, or not even realize that he lost. As opposed to having second best cards at a table game the two of you Rasp may agree that they have both gained ....something. This is a great option, especially if you're talking to family and friends!

In expanding the topics in a negotiation, you stand an opportunity to generate worth that is greater than when you were focusing upon the single, primary problem. When you, along with Rasp appreciate the incremental aspects or products differently, by mixing concessions on these concerns, both of you will gain more value from your investment than if you just tried to settle the first question.

The perception of value disparity is what makes the difference. Everyday, we have the chance to see the different ways people value things. We must however be attentive to utilize the difference in value in negotiations. It isn't always valued in the eyes of Rasp in the sense that it is worth nearly as high as what you've valued it. Therefore, he might offer the concession as a reward for a different concession, which may be considered to be insignificant to you, yet crucial for him. When you mix concessions to enhance the value of their combined effect, you as well as Rasp are able to generate value that is perceived. The perceived value instead of the worth of each commodity to create a win-win.

If Rasp considers a concession made on your part as significant, you don't have a reason to claim that you think the concession to be a minor one. Keep in mind to keep your fake smile and feign discomfort. The essence of negotiation is in the perception of creating worth, which means that all parties could feel a stake in the final outcome. When you as well as Rasp are both feeling like winners following the conclusion of an agreement you are both happy with and Rasp, all the more. These agreements will likely stay in force when the two parties exchange handshakes and leave.

Creating value is work. It takes knowledge, planning as well as inspiration. But the reward could be a mutually beneficial solution.

Conflict can arise in situations where two or more persons contest over the value of a item. The land, the money, woman or a male, the baseball bat, or the final piece of cake can all create conflict if availability is not as abundant or believed as being. One solution to this conflict beyond the force of arms or bartering to get an item in particular is to reach a mutual understanding regarding the re-alignment of interest across a variety of related goods and services through strategic concessions in order to come to an agreement on the main goal. This strategy should be effective even in modern times, in the event that the item will be the focus of one's heart and conflicts are against a rival. When emotions prevail, it can result in boys becoming embarrassed before their entire school and even less so the person they want to be using ill-conceived methods intended to make a statement!

Negotiations are taking place. It broadens the scope of discussions to allow both parties to gradually enhance the value of group commodities by allocating every concession to the person which is the one who value it most. This means that you'll be valuing items 1 3 7, and 9 at a higher rates over Rasp and Rasp is likely to value items 2 4 5 and 10 at her highest worth. If you take to the "high-value" rates of items 1 to 10 in this manner, it will be perceived to have more value than had the other of you Rasp to evaluate the ten things on their own. If you are able to construct an agreement based on the inflated value, you be able to add value creatively through negotiation. By doing this, you'll be capable of satisfying the apparent requirements for Rasp enough to merit an agreement to be reached. This is due to the disparity between the value you attach to the importance of things and what Rasp is able to do.

It is sometimes challenging to provide value. When the goal of the conflict is extremely limited, like when an armed robber intends on getting your money in a dark corner there is a chance for adding value and align your interest is evidently very limited. In some instances, the best choice is to be able to discern superior power and offer the wallet in exchange to be able to walk away unharmed. The robbers are counting on this. He is calculating that you will give up the cash, rather than risk the safety of your family. The focus of the conflict is specific and the decision you make ought to be easy and, at the very least, it should seem to most people.

When the goal of negotiations is broadened the opportunities could arise to generate value, due to the potential difference in perceived worth.

Value disparity is the most important factor in enhancing value. Because we're all different We value things differently. In the event that you Rasp both agree to give up a thing while receiving something different for it, the worth of the transaction could be enhanced to both you and Rasp. A different view of things allows for the pairing of exchanges or concessions which have potential to increase the worth of all products.

A spare hammer holds little value for its owner, a carpenter as compared for a carpenter who does not have a Hammer. The one who has redundancy or backup through the spare hammer, while the second is off the market until he has the new hammer.

Similar to a conflict about a small issue between a contractor and a client, an apology from the contractor could bring about a major concession from the client. The price of an apology for the company is an act of self-promotion The reward for the apology is money that is cold and hard.

SEPARATING THE PRIMARY GOAL FROM THE OBJECTIVES

Negotiations are all about the concept in the form of "consideration." What, what, and how you provide consideration are the essence of negotiation. The term "consideration" in negotiations refers to everything that is valuable to a participant. Most commonly used types of consideration include:

Money, hard currency or cash.

Some tangible assets, such as property or any other that has intrinsic worth.

Power, position or power, position or

Entertainment, Sex or even love.

Allegiance or Support.

A few of your assets could be much less value for your personal needs than Rasp. Sailboats can be like that. A seller may have enjoyed their vessel for a long time, but would like to make improvements and is looking for an upgrade to a larger, more spacious vessel. The worth of the old vessel for the seller could be lower than buyers, especially those who is in to the boat could be willing to spend. There's an emotional component in how we evaluate or value our possessions. If it's something we desire, it's likely to be more valuable for us than the time we own it or looking to sell it. It is an emotional value.

If you're looking to earn most money from your older boat, it is important to look for ways to add worth to the sale. One example is not including the dinghy as part of the cost of acquiring the boat. There is a possibility to transfer the dinghy's ownership to an outside party, but not reduce the cost of your sailboat. The buyer may be expecting other items, including the dinghy for a bargain, however that doesn't necessarily mean that they'll quit if they don't receive the item. They want the sailboat that they are looking for but not the Dinghy.

By dissolving commodities, you will be able to increase the value of your product to benefit you. The worth of the boat to those who are looking for the dinghy or another potential buyer may be considered a distinct purchase. If you put it for sale as an individual commodity, you could be able to increase the value the dinghy, by requiring the buyer to appraise it according to market value instead of discounting its worth as part of a bigger transaction. If you do your homework there is a chance that you will get in the lead.

If you are tempted to add the dinghy an incentive for a hesitant purchaser of the sailboat take care when making this offer. If you offer the dinghy when you're waiting for the buyer to come decision on an initial price to purchase the vessel, this could suggest that you do not value the boat at the price you are offering. Like every concession, the time of the concession is crucial. Utilizing your assets in line with this value gap allows you to increase the net profit you get from negotiations.

Expert negotiators, arbitrators, and mediators are aware of aspects of a dispute that aren't tangible yet may hold immense value for either or both of the parties. They are nevertheless currency in the course of a transaction. Simple words of apology from you could prompt Rasp to consent to unacceptable financial conditions. The exchange of a different consideration is also a source of worth. Utilizing this kind of intangible currencies is a fundamental method of negotiation.

In the event of an argument or dispute, it's natural and normal to feel driven by your goals and targets. However, it may not be enough for you to agree. One reason for being at odds with Rasp is that you do not want the same things Rasp does or her desires. Your desires are at odds. It is a need to get the item, and not the winning of the debate itself. The issue is what costs it would cost to achieve what you need. The final deal is only a way to reach an agreement. The terms will be important for the parties.

Family, social or personal conflicts can place you in the position as a negotiator (directly in the process) and mediator (settling disputes between other people). If you discover that you are thrust to the position of mediator, it's important to recognize that the roles are very similar, but they differ. There are different fundamentals. Each is seeking to create an agreement. This goal, forming some sort of agreement is the main objective of a mediator who is attempting to resolve disputes between other parties. In your role as a mediator, but not a judge, or jury member, you're not as concerned about the fairness or justice of having all the factions that have been fighting to settle and put their differences to rest. Being a mediator, it is likely that you'll only be at a glance interested in the details of the agreement since the mediator's role is over once the deal is signed.

Chapter 5: Understanding Arguments in Relationships

Beautiful but they can be super challenging, especially when it comes to arguments and your own EGO. When it comes to relationships, conflict and disagreements are a part of the process However, how couples deal with their disagreements could be the difference between the quality of their relationship. Conflicts within relationships could create a stronger bond or even tear them apart, based on the manner in which they manage them.

In the first section, we'll explore the basic arguments that are involved within relationships. This includes defining arguments, the common triggers for argument, as well as negative consequences of unresolved argument.

Defining Arguments

A disagreement is one among two or more persons with a disagreement over beliefs, opinions or convictions. The arguments in relationships may take place in a variety of ways including disagreements regarding finances, family and work options.

In the majority of cases, disputes between couples occur due to the fact that they are able to have differing views on the issue at hand, and they're trying to find common ground in order to settle the matter. Arguments can be constructive, or damaging, depending on how couples deal with their disagreements.

Engaging in constructive arguments is beneficial for relationships because they allow couples the chance to share their thoughts and views, share their concerns as well as desires and, ultimately discover a solution to the issues that is at hand. Disruptive arguments, on contrary, could cause serious damage to relationships, which can lead to anger, resentment and breakups.

Common Triggers of Arguments

Disputs within relationships may occur due to a range of triggers. The most common triggers are:

1. Insufficient communication is the pillar of any positive relationship. If couples do not communicate well, conflicts and conflict can develop and lead to disputes.

2. Different beliefs and values: Couples come from different cultures and hold different opinions as well as values. This can result in disputes and conflict, in particular when couples refuse to compromise, or even respect one the other's views.

3. Stress: Stressful situations related to work, like stress as well as financial problems, medical issues, could result in arguments within relationships. When couples are stressed out, they are likely to be more irritable, less patient and more likely fight.

4. Unfulfilled expectations: When it comes to marriage, couples usually are able to set expectations for one another. If these expectations aren't satisfied, it may result in frustration and disappointment which can lead to arguments.

5. Jealousy: It is often the cause of disputes in relationships, specifically those who feel insecure or frightened by another's behaviors or actions.

The Negative Impact of Unresolved Arguments

Disagreements that cannot be resolved may affect negatively relationships. If a couple fails to solve the issues, it could result in anger, resentment as well as break-ups in the relationship. A few of the negative consequences that result from unresolved disagreements are:

1. Insecurity: Unsolved disputes can cause distrust between partners, which makes it hard for couples to trust each other.

2. Couples who are emotionally distant cannot resolve disagreements, it may result in emotional discord and disconnection from the relationships.

3. Problems with health: Conflicts that are not resolved could cause stress, anxiety as well as depression. All of which could affect the physical as well as mental well-being.

4. Unable to settle future disputes In the event that couples are not able to come to an agreement and conflicts, they can result in an environment of conflict within the marriage. This makes it challenging for them to settle new conflicts.

As a conclusion, disagreements are the normal part of every relationship. How couples manage the arguments they have can make the difference to the outcome of their relationships. Knowing the causes of disagreements and the detrimental impact on relationships that are not resolved is vital to establishing healthy relationships. In the next section we'll explore the most the most effective methods of handling disputes within relationships, such as communicating, active listening and compromise.

Chapter 6: Communication in Relationships

Communication is essential to the success for any good relationship. Couples can communicate their desires and emotions as well as understand one another's viewpoints and, ultimately, create a lasting and enjoyable connection. In this section we'll explore the significance of effective communication during relationships. This includes engaging listening and non-verbal communications.

Effective Communication

Effective communication requires two ways. This involves talking and paying attention. When couples are able to communicate effectively and effectively, they can convey their ideas and emotions in a clear and concise manner, free of judgment or resentment. Additionally, they are able to comprehend and understand the other's perspective, which will help them come up with solutions to their issues.

One key to effective communication is the use of "I" statements instead of "you" statements. "I" statements allow couples to voice their opinions and feelings views without blaming the other person. As an example, instead of declaring "You never listen to me," the more efficient strategy is "I feel unheard when we argue."

A key aspect of successful communicating is assertiveness, however, not overly aggressive. In assertiveness, you are able to express your thoughts and feelings in a concise and courteous way. In contrast, aggression however is when you blame or attack your companion, which may increase arguments and damage to your relationship.

Importance of Active Listening

Listening actively is an essential element of effective communication relationships. It requires you to focus on what your spouse is saying without interruptions or interruptions. Engaging in active listening can help couples comprehend each other's views and validate their feelings and finally, discover solutions for their issues.

The key to active listening is to give your partner all your concentration. That means getting rid of all distractions like smartphones or laptops while focusing completely on what your partner's words. Also, it is important to avoid interruptions such as not the end of your partner's sentence or chiming in with your thinking.

Another crucial element of active listening is asking questions that clarify the relationship. These questions can help couples be able to fully comprehend each other's viewpoints and emotions. You could, for instance, say, "Can you tell me more about how you're feeling?" Or "What do you mean when you say that?"

Nonverbal Communication

Nonverbal communication is ways of communicating without the use of words.

This includes gestures of the face, body language and the tone of voice. Communication through nonverbal means is as crucial as communication through verbs within relationships because it communicates emotions and feelings that words can't.

A very crucial elements of nonverbal communications in a relationship is eye contact. Eye contact signals to your companion that you're fully involved and present in discussion. This also aids in conveying confidence and trust.

Another crucial aspect that is non-verbal communications is the body language. The body language conveys emotions and sentiments which words cannot convey. Like, for instance cross-arms can indicate defensiveness or lack of mind Leaning towards could signal interest and commitment.

Effective communication is at the heart for a healthy relationship. Communication involves speaking and being attentive, making use of "I" statements instead of "you" statements, being active but not aggressive while being attentive to your partner's viewpoint. The nonverbal way of communicating, for example eyes and body language are just as crucial as the verbal method of communicating emotions and thoughts. In the next section we'll explore ways couples can make use of efficient communication and active listening to settle disputes and conflicts between them.

Chapter 7: Identifying Your Communication Style

Communication in relationships that is effective isn't just about how you speak and how you say it. The way you communicate will have an effect on the way your partner thinks of you and, ultimately your success in your relationship. In this section we'll explore three communication styles that are common that are assertive, passive and aggressive. We will also give you a quick survey to assist you in identifying your style of communication.

Assertive Communication

The term "assertive" refers to a communication technique that requires you to communicate your feelings and thoughts with a clear and courteous way. This allows you to express your desires and needs without blaming or attacking the other person. Communication that is assertive is defined by the utilization of "I" statements, active listening, and an ability to accept compromise.

Communication experts who are assertive communicate their thoughts and emotions clearly and in a concise style, while not minimising or overstating their feelings. They also pay attention to their counterpart's viewpoint and help them come up with solutions that satisfy each of their requirements. Communicators who assert themselves are also more willing to negotiate and come up with an agreement, which can help to create a more enduring and healthier relationships.

Passive Communication

The term "passive" refers to a method of communication that focuses on the avoidance of conflict, or sharing your feelings and thoughts. The majority of passive communicators minimize their personal needs and wants as well as accept their partners' requirements to keep from conflicts. This may lead to feelings of anger and frustration since passive listeners might feel that their personal requirements are not being met.

People who are passive may have difficulties expressing their emotions and thoughts that can cause mistakes and confusion. Some may struggle in active listening because they might be concerned with avoiding conflict rather than being able to comprehend their partner's viewpoint.

Aggressive Communication

Agressive communication refers to the type of communication that involves attacking or blameing your partner for achieving the results you desire. The most aggressive communicators will often employ "you" statements instead of "I" statements, and can interrupt or talk over their partners to establish their authority.

Communication that is aggressive can cause damage for relationships because it may cause feelings of anger and hurt. This can lead to the breakdown of communication because the attention is shifted away from finding solutions and instead focusing on blaming the blame.

Identifying Your Communication Style

For help in identifying the style of communication you use, fill out the survey below:

1. In the event of a dispute between you and your companion, should you

a. Communicate your thoughts and feelings with respect and in a clear way? b. Be wary of conflict, or communicate your emotions and thoughts by avoiding confrontation? 3. Criticize or blame your spouse to gain the results you desire?

2. If your spouse or partner is expressing their opinions and emotions, will you?

a. Pay attention and comprehend their viewpoint? b. Try to minimize their feelings or to keep conflict out of the equation? 3. Disrupt them or discuss them to establish your authority?

3. In the event that you must compromise with your spouse, will you:

A. Willing to seek an agreement and then work toward an outcome that is in line with each of your requirements? b. Accept the demands of your spouse in order to prevent conflict? C. Resist accept compromises and insist on obtaining what you want?

If the majority of your answers were A's, you probably are a confident communicator. It is an appropriate and effective style of communication which can assist you in building an effective and satisfying relationship.

If you responded mostly with B's and a few A's, you may possess a passive style of communication. The way you communicate may cause anger and feelings of frustration which may need some effort to be more assertive with your communications.

If your answers are mostly C's, you may are a bit aggressive in your communication. The way you communicate could be detrimental to relationships, and could require assistance from a professional to resolve.

The way you communicate has a major effect on the overall success and longevity of the relationship. Affirmative communication is a positive and efficient communication method which allows you to communicate your wishes and requirements in a respectful and direct way, all while actively taking in your partner's viewpoint and figuring out solutions that satisfy each of your requirements. In contrast, passive communication in contrast is a source of anger or resentment and also a break in communications. A shrewd communication is damaging to relationships, and could cause hurt feelings and distrust.

When you recognize your preferred style of communication and working to become more assertive with your communications You can enhance relationships as well as increase happiness with your loved ones. Effective communication requires more than simply speaking, it is a matter of attentive listening as well as nonverbal communication and the willingness to compromise. With these tools and strategies, you will be able to effectively argue with your spouse and not cause significant harm to the relationship.

Chapter 8: Identifying Your Partner's Communication Style

Effective communication is at the heart of a healthy relationship. It is important to recognize that no one communicates the same manner, and this may lead to misunderstandings or arguments that can cause damaging the relationship. It is crucial to recognize your partner's communications manner so that you better comprehend them and help them efficiently communicate.

Observing Communication Patterns

The first step to determine the style of communication your partner uses is to watch their patterns of communication. Be aware of how they talk to your partner, their tone of and body language as well as the language they employ. Do they speak clearly and clearly do they communicate clearly and assertively, or are they inactive and evasive? Are they using humor or sarcasm in order to diffuse disputes, or make it worse?

Recognizing Triggers

Triggers are situations or events that could lead to argument or disputes in a relationship. If you can identify your spouse's triggers they can be avoided or deal with these situations in a way which minimizes conflict. Common triggers are the stress of finances, jealousy, fear of being judged, different parenting style, or disputes over chores in the home. Recognizing the triggers of your partner can aid you in managing them successfully.

Understanding Different Communication Styles

There are three primary communications styles: assertive active, and passive like we've covered in the last chapter. Each is defined by distinct behaviors and approaches in communication.

Identifying Your Partner's Communication Style

When you've analyzed the patterns of communication between your partners and have identified the triggers that they use, it's crucial to comprehend the way they communicate. It's possible to do this by having a transparent and open conversation by asking what they prefer and how they handle conflict. Additionally, it can be beneficial by taking a brief survey to discover your communication preferences and the triggers.

Short Survey: Identifying Your Partner's Communication Style

Here are a few questions that will assist you in identifying your spouse's style of communication. Be honest and share your responses with your friend.

1. In the event of a conflict with your spouse, do they have a tendency to:

a. Communicate their desires and needs in a respectful and direct approach? b. Refrain from conflict, or express their concerns in an indirect manner? 3. Communicate their concerns with a threatening or hurtful or hurtful

2. In your conversations with your spouse, are they:

a. Pay attention and get your thoughts across? b. Get defensive or tune out? C. Disrupt or minimize your viewpoint?

3. In the event that they're unhappy or angry, do they?

a. Be able to express their feelings with respect and calm manner? b. Refrain from the expression of their feelings? 3. express their feelings with a style that's rude or hurtful to you?

4. When they need some thing from you, can they

a. Communicate their desires and needs clearly and in a direct method? b. Make a ruse or employ passive-aggressive behaviors in order to obtain what they need? 3. Use threats or demands to obtain the results they desire?

5. If they resolve conflicts, do they:

a. Find a compromise that is beneficial for both sides? b. Refrain from conflict by submitting to your personal preferences? 3. Remain insistent on the way they want, regardless of what you want?

If you answer these questions by discussing your answers to gain a more understanding of your companion's manner of communication and learn how to effectively interact with them.

Being aware of your partner's personality is crucial to establishing a good communication within a relationship. If you can observe their patterns of communication and recognizing the triggers they use, and understanding how they communicate and triggers, you will be able to be more effective in communicating with them and avoid conflict. Effective communication is crucial for a successful and satisfying marriage By taking the time to observe and appreciate your partner's communications manner, you can create a an even stronger and satisfying relationships.

Chapter 9: Understanding Emotional Intelligence

The term "emotional intelligence" refers to the capacity to recognize the impact of, control, and communicate your own feelings in addition to being able to identify and react appropriately to emotional state of other people. The ability to express emotions is a crucial aspect of successful communication relationships. It is able to assist couples in navigating conflict effectively and in a positive method.

In this section we'll look at the notion of emotional intelligence. We will also explore ways you can improve the skills of emotional intelligence to increase your communication and problem-solving skills within your relationships. In this chapter, we will concentrate on three main aspects of emotional intelligence namely the ability to recognize emotions, managing them as well as the ability to empathize.

Emotional Self-Awareness

The term "emotional self-awareness" is the capacity to understand and recognize the emotions you experience. The development of emotional self-awareness will assist you in establishing a more effective communication with your loved ones and aid you with managing the emotions you experience during conflict. These are some methods to help you improve your awareness of your emotions:

1. Mindfulness Meditation: The practice of mindfulness is focused attention on the present moment while observing your emotions and thoughts with no judgment. It can assist you to be more conscious of your mood and assist you in controlling your feelings during conflict.

2. Journaling writing about your feelings and thoughts will help you be more conscious of your emotions. It is possible to use a journal to reflect on your experiences and observe trends in your emotional reactions.

3. Self-Reflection: Make moments each morning to consider your feelings and their impact on the way you behave. It can assist you in becoming more conscious of your triggers for emotion and help manage the emotions you experience during conflicts.

Managing Emotions

The ability to manage emotions requires the ability to control your emotional state and to respond accordingly to other people's emotions. Below are some suggestions to manage your feelings during conflict:

1. Pause: If you are overwhelmed by your feelings during a dispute You should take a break in order to clear your mind. It can assist you in not taking a decision or action that you regret later.

2. Learn to practice active listening: Focusing on what your companion says without interjecting or displaying defensiveness. It can assist you in managing your emotions, helping you understand the

viewpoint of your friend and respond in a manner that is appropriate.

3. Make use of "I" Statements: Using "I" statements can help to express your feelings without threatening. In other words Instead of using the phrase "You always do this," use the phrase "I feel upset when this happens."

Empathy

Empathy refers to the ability to be aware of and react to others' emotions. The development of empathy will help you recognize your partner's point of view as they fight and also aid in communicating more effectively. These are some methods to develop empathy

1. Learn to practice active listening: Focusing on what your companion says without interrupting them or getting defensive. It can aid you in understanding the perspective of your partner and react in a manner that is appropriate.

2. Try to imagine yourself in their shoes Imagine the way your loved one feels and the emotions they're experiencing. It can aid you in developing empathy, and react to the feelings of your partner with compassion.

3. Validate their Feelings: Validating the partner's feelings involves acknowledging what they feel and showing compassion. As an example, saying "I understand why you are feeling upset" will make your partner feel more respected and valued.

Learning to develop emotional intelligence will assist you in developing a more effective communication with your spouse and assist you in navigating disputes in a safe and efficient manner. When you develop self-awareness about your emotions as well as managing your emotions and gaining empathy, you will be able to build the foundation for a more satisfying and stronger connection with your loved one. Keep in mind that gaining emotional intelligence is a process that takes some time and effort, however the advantages of enhancing the skills of your emotional intelligence will be worth it.

Chapter 10: Identifying and Managing Emotions during Arguments

It is important to consider emotions in disputes with your partner. If you're feeling emotional and you're in a rush, it's easy to become caught up with the emotion of the moment, and make things we're not meant to. It can cause significant harm to relationships. It is therefore essential to be aware of and manage your the emotions that arise during disputes to avoid the damage.

Recognizing Triggers

The first step is to recognize triggers. stage in regulating emotional reactions during disagreements. Triggers refer to circumstances or incidents that trigger an emotional response either in your spouse or you. They can range including a tone of voice or a specific subject of discussion.

It is essential to recognize your triggers as well as your partner's triggers in order to stay clear of fierce arguments. If you are aware that an issue may be sensitive to your spouse be sure to steer clear of the topic or proceed in a cautious manner. Also, if you realize the tone or voice of your partner's tone of voice, you should try to remain calm and do not to react instantly.

Managing Your Reactions to Partner's Emotions

It's not uncommon for one person's feelings to trigger another partner's feelings. In the case of anger, if one person is angry and the other party is angry, they could also be upset in reaction. It can result in an unending cycle of rising feelings.

But, it's crucial to realize that you're the sole responsible for your emotions and your reactions. It is impossible to control the spouse's mood however, you are able to control your responses to these emotions. If you notice that your spouse is angry don't instantly react. Instead, you should take time to relax and evaluate the circumstances. When you're relaxed and calm, you'll be able to respond to the situation in a way that's positive and can help to ease tension.

De-escalating Tension

If emotions are high It is crucial to reduce tension in order to stop an argument from spiralling beyond control. An effective method to lessen tension is to stop for a moment. If you are feeling like you are having a heated conversation take an interruption from the discussion. It gives the other person and you some time to cool down and think about the issue.

In the time between breaks It is important to take a moment to reflect on your emotions and responses. You should think about the triggers that triggered your emotions and the reason. This will help you improve your emotional control in any future disagreements.

It's equally important to bring back to the discussion once both of you are in a calm state. During your conversation, make sure to concentrate on the topic that is at hand, and refrain from bringing back past disputes or irrelevant concerns. Keep your focus on finding solutions to the issue.

Controlling your emotions when you are in a heated argument can be crucial to maintaining the health and happiness of your relation with your spouse. Being aware of the triggers, directing your responses to the emotions of your partner as well as defusing tension the most important skills you can have for managing the emotions that arise during disputes.

It is important to keep in mind that emotions are normal and are normal. It's normal to feel emotions. But, it's crucial to control them properly so that you don't cause significant harm for your relationships. Through practice and perseverance you will acquire the abilities needed to control your emotions successfully and be able to have constructive arguments with your partner.

Chapter 11: Understanding the Importance

Can be hard to apologize particularly in the context of a disagreement between you and your spouse Apologizing is, however, crucial to maintaining good relationships. Knowing how to express your apology in a sincere manner and take responsibility to your behavior, and accept your partner's forgiveness will help you avoid arguments damaging your relationship in a significant way.

Sincere Apologies

An honest apology means accepting responsibility for your actions, confessing regret as well as taking the necessary steps to rectify the issue. One of the first steps in giving an honest apology is admitting your mistakes. It's not easy to acknowledge fault, but it's essential to move towards a better future.

The next step is to express regret to the extent that your conduct hurt the relationship between you and your partner. It could be as simple as acknowledging the pain or anger they could be experiencing, or providing reassurances that you'll improve in the near future. Avoid making excuses or trying to minimize the consequences on your conduct.

Then, you must take action to correct the situation. It could involve drafting an action plan to stop similar mistakes from occurring next time or offering to amend the situation by some means or asking your friend what they want from you to make progress.

Importance of Accountability

Being accountable for your conduct is a crucial element of a genuine apology. The concept of accountability is acknowledging that choices have consequences and you are obligated to fulfill the obligation to put the right choices.

If you are accountable to your choices, you show to your spouse that you're ready to own your errors and take steps to avoid them next time around. This will help build trust and stop future conflicts.

Forgiveness

The power of forgiveness is in preventing disputes from causing serious harm. When you are able to forgive your partner and let off any bitterness or resentment you are looking for, and permit you to go forward positively.

It can be difficult to forgive particularly if you partner has been a major source of pain. But, it's an essential element of a healthy relationship, which can prevent disputes from becoming more intense and creating permanent destruction.

It is crucial to remember that forgiveness is not absolving or denying the actions of your partner. It is more about acknowledging that the person you love is human, and every person has their own mistakes. It is a decision which can be challenging to choose, however it could also be extremely beneficial.

If you want to be able to forgiving your partner It is essential to speak openly and truthfully about how their behavior has had an impact on you. It is also important to cooperate to restore confidence and stop similar mistakes to occur in the future.

Arguments are element of relationships however, they don't necessarily have to result in significant harm. If you are aware of the importance of apology, acknowledging responsibility to your conduct as well as practicing forgiveness it is possible to prevent disputes in the future from growing into a cause of lasting injury.

It is essential to engage in the argument with understanding, empathy as well as a desire to be open and willing to learn from your counterpart. If you can identify your preferred communication style as well as recognizing triggers and controlling your anger during debates to prevent disputes that turn into a full-blown argument.

In addition, by developing the art of emotional intelligence, you will be able to learn to better comprehend your emotions and behave with more sanity in arguments. Through practice and commitment it is possible to acquire the necessary skills to be able to debate with your partner without doing any harm, and develop a stronger healthy, more harmonious relationships as a result.

Chapter 12: Conflict Resolution Techniques

In every relationship, conflict can be a part of the equation. There are no two individuals identical, so it's normal for people to have their own perspectives and views. But how couples deal with conflicts can have an enormous influence on the quality and durability of their relationships. In this article we'll look at three strategies for resolving conflict that include compromise, negotiation and collaboration. In addition, we will give examples of best practices.

Compromise

A common strategy for resolving conflict that involves seeking a compromise that is acceptable to two sides. The process requires both sides to compromise in order to arrive at an agreeable solution. It is usually thought of as a quick and easy solution to settle disputes, however it may also result in feelings of resentment when one person feels that they're always having to make sacrifices.

A good example of a best practice Sarah and John are trying to figure out which place to visit during their holiday. Sarah prefers to head to the beach, whereas John prefers mountains. After a lengthy discussion and their respective preferences, they agree to agree to go to an area with a lake where they will be able to enjoy both the beaches and mountains.

Negotiation

Negotiation is another strategy which can prove successful in solving conflicts. In contrast to compromise, negotiations involve each party making efforts to listen to each other's wants and issues. Negotiation requires honesty and open dialogue and an openness to come up with the best solution for both sides.

A good example of good practice Kelly and Mike have been trying to determine what chores they should share in their household. Kelly prefers washing clothes, however, Mike prefers to do the dishes. They agree to bargain and devise the system in which Kelly takes care of the laundry while Mike is the one to wash dishes, and they each alternate cleaning their bathroom and vacuuming.

Collaboration

Collaboration requires working in tandem to come up with the best solution to meet each partner's needs. It demands a great deal of empathy and communication since both sides must be able to comprehend the other's perspective and come up with an approach that is beneficial to each other equally.

A good example of good practice Maria and Juan are trying to figure out the best way to spend their time. Maria would like to spend the night out with her group of friends, whereas Juan would prefer to stay in and watch a flick. They agree to work together and create an arrangement where they meet up with their acquaintances on a Saturday night and then sit at home and watch a film on Sunday.

Conflict is an integral element of every relationship However, how couples deal with conflicts can make all the differences. Through techniques such as compromise negotiations, compromise, and collaboration couples can discover solutions that will meet both partners' requirements, and also strengthen their relationships. It's important to keep in mind that working through conflicts requires practice as well as both parties must agree in order to come up with an outcome that is beneficial to both parties.

Chapter 13: Managing Power Struggles

Conflicts over power are an incredibly common aspect of relationships. When a partner believes that they are in more control or control over one of the others, it could result in resentment and even conflicts. In this article we'll look at various ways the imbalance of power can impact relationships. We will also provide suggestions to manage power conflicts.

Recognizing Power Imbalances

Power imbalances can manifest through a variety of ways within the course of a relationship. A couple may be able to benefit from more money, status in society and decision-making power. It is crucial that couples recognize the imbalances in power and the potential effects they could have on their relationship.

An example of a power imbalance occurs where one of the partners is the main breadwinner of the marriage. It can create an unbalanced situation in which the other person feels dependent on main earner, and could have lesser influence in the financial decision-making process. Another scenario could be when the dominant partner is one of the persona or assumes greater responsibility within the relationship which leaves one partner feeling helpless.

Balancing Power in Relationships

In a partnership, balancing power is the key to avoid conflict of interests. This requires finding ways to distribute the decision-making power and responsibility equally between the partners. Balance of power can be accomplished through open communications as well as compromise and negotiation.

The first step is to open up communication. step in creating a balance of power in the relationship. Each partner must be willing to be open to listening to one another's opinions and concerns. This is possible by regular meetings, in which both partners sit down to share how they're doing and discuss the areas that are causing concern.

The concept of compromise is another important strategy to balance power in relationships. It involves negotiating an acceptable compromise that both parties will be willing to compromise in order to arrive at a mutually agreeable resolution. The need for compromise is typically needed when both parties are in conflict or have differing needs.

Negotiation is an efficient method of balancing the power. Both parties must make efforts to learn about the other's concerns and needs and negotiating an outcome that is beneficial to both sides. Negotiation demands open and honest dialogue and an openness to come up with an answer that is compatible with each of the parties' requirements.

Managing Power Struggles During Arguments

The power struggles that arise can occur in the course of arguments and can have detrimental consequences for the relationships. Couples need to acknowledge these struggles and manage the issue effectively.

A good way to manage the power struggle during arguments is to stop as things get more heated. The best way to do this is to step away from the debate for a short period of time or even removing yourself entirely from the argument. It allows the parties to relax and view an argument from a objective standpoint.

Another option is to concentrate on listening actively. This means making a conscious effort to be able to comprehend the perspective of another person and not interrupting or getting defensive. Being active in your listening will help each partner be heard and respected this can decrease the chance of conflict between power players.

It's also crucial for couples not to use words that can create the power imbalances. It could be as simple as using derogatory phrases, making assumptions about the motives of the other and speaking with the tone of a snarky. A language that exacerbates the power imbalance could escalate disputes and create a greater challenge to come to a conclusion.

Conflicts over power can lead to a lot of tension in relationships. When couples recognize power imbalances as well as balancing power within the marriage, and resolving the power struggle during disputes couples are able to avoid detrimental consequences, and build their bond. It is crucial for each partner to play part in balancing the power dynamics, and work towards an enlightened relationships.

Chapter 14: Managing Differences in Relationships

There are no two individuals identical, so in every relationship there will some variations. The differences could lead to tension if not handled properly. In this section we'll explore ways to manage differences within relationships. This includes acknowledging different perspectives, respecting boundaries and reaching a compromise.

Celebrating Differences

Different interests, values as well as personalities makes each individual unique. If partners acknowledge each other's individuality, it will result in a more positive relationship. It is about acknowledging and embracing one another's individuality and finding ways to acknowledge each other's unique qualities.

A great way to acknowledge different aspects is to learn about the interests of each other. It could mean trying out different hobbies or activities that each partner is interested in. Additionally, it could involve knowing about one another's culture and customs.

Another method of celebrating different aspects is to highlight the strengths of each other. This could mean taking note of and appreciating one another's strengths and abilities. The partners can also collaborate to help each other out in the areas in which one of them might be weaker than the other.

Respecting Boundaries

Respecting boundaries between each other is vital to manage differences in relationships. Boundaries define personal limitations as well as expectations regarding how the couples should behave towards one another. When people respect one another's limits, it results in an improved and happier relationships.

A way to set boundaries and maintain them is through an open and transparent conversations. It involves discussing the other's requirements and expectations regarding the relationship. The partners can also establish the boundaries of the privacy of their personal space, times and privacy.

A different way of respecting limits is to stay clear of crossing boundaries. This could mean asking permission prior to sharing any personal data or taking decisions that may be detrimental to the person who is making them. Partner can also refrain from pushing their partners to agree on things they don't like or are do not feel ready for.

Finding Common Ground

The search for the common ground is a crucial method to manage differences within relationships. It involves identifying the areas in which both partners have common desires or beliefs and building upon the areas of common interest.

Additionally, it can involve making compromises that are beneficial to each of the partners.

A way to come up with the common ground is by focusing on common goals. The process can include sharing your goals in the near future, and then finding ways to work together towards achieving each others' objectives. The two partners can work in order to reach common goals, like saving up to take a trip or setting out to achieve a common goal for their careers.

Another method of finding the common ground is to concentrate on the common values. The process can include discussing your beliefs and principles and incorporating those beliefs into your partnership. The partners can also collaborate to promote causes or concerns which are significant for both parties.

Example of Good Practice

John as well as Jane have been together for some time. They're different people with distinct preferences and personalities and this has caused certain conflicts over the years. But, they've learned to deal with their differences through taking them as a blessing, while respecting each their boundaries and to find the common ground.

John is an introvert who likes to read and spend time with his own company. Jane tends to be more active and is a lover of being with relatives and friends. To honor their distinct personalities They have decided to share the responsibility of planning events which they both enjoy. It has resulted in them exploring new ideas as well as learning about each their interests.

Both John as well as Jane both have established distinct boundaries for their private space and times. John enjoys peace and quiet and Jane appreciates his need for privacy. Jane enjoys spending moments with her buddies and John appreciates the need for her to maintain a social existence.

Then, John and Jane have discovered a commonality in their principles. They are both committed to being a part of the community. They have also begun working with a local charity with each other. They share a love for the outdoors and have set the goal to discover new trails for hiking.

Chapter 15: Handling Financial Disagreements

It is one of the main causes of conflicts within relationships. It is a delicate subject that causes different views, beliefs as well as priorities. With the proper techniques, couples can be taught how to resolve their differences concerning money in a healthy and healthy manner.

Identifying Differences in Attitudes Towards Money

The first step to manage disputes about money is to determine any difference in the way people view money exists between the spouses. This means understanding the one's views, beliefs as well as priorities in relation to money.

One partner, for instance, might be more focused in saving money for the future and the other might be more focused on living in the present. One partner could be more cautious in the area of investing, whereas the other partner might be more inclined to take on risks.

If they can understand the differences between them Partners can cooperate in a way which is beneficial to each of them. This could mean setting common objectives and goals including saving up to pay for a downpayment on the house or repaying the debt.

Budgeting Strategies

After identifying the differences between their attitudes toward finances, the next thing to do is to create an effective budgeting plan that is suitable for them both. It is the process of creating a strategy that will guide them in managing the money they have on a day-today basis.

There are many budgeting techniques that couples may utilize. The most popular is to use the envelope method in which partners assign a set amount of cash to various groups (such like entertainment, food as well as transportation) and then keep it in different envelopes.

A different strategy is the 50/30/20 rule. In this case, the majority of your earnings are allocated to essential expenses (such such as housing, food transport, etc.)) while 30% is put aside for discretionary expenses (such as entertainment or eating out) while 20% goes towards saving as well as debt repayment.

Long-Term Financial Planning

Alongside the day-to-day budgeting techniques, couples must think about the longer-term financial planning. The process involves setting targets for the future like saving money for retirement, or planning the education of a child.

A key aspect of financial planning over the long run is preparing an emergency savings. It should be able to provide funds to pay for at least three or six months of expenses in the event the loss of employment or an unexpected cost.

Another element of planning for long-term financial success is planning for retirement. The partners should collaborate in setting a retirement target to determine how much they must save every month to meet this goal, then choose the right investments to meet their personal risk tolerance as well as goals.

Here are a few examples of best practices for managing financial disagreements:

1. Communication that is honest and open The partners should be transparent and honest with one another about their financial position along with their financial goals and the issues they face. It is also important to discuss the debts, incomes or other expenses that could affect their financial situation.

2. Flexibility and compromise: Partners are expected to make compromises and remain

open to controlling their financial affairs. It could mean finding innovative solutions that are beneficial for both of them, like creating a budget that permits the possibility of spending some money on discretionary expenses.

3. Check-ins on a regular basis: Partners must periodically check in with each with the goal of ensuring that they're within their financial objectives. It could involve review of their budgets, tracking the amount they spend, or discussing any change in their financial position.

4. Get help from a professional When partners struggle to control their finances or are having significant disagreements regarding money, they might be interested in consulting counsellors or financial planners. They can offer advice as well as assistance with managing financial matters and in resolving disputes.

To conclude, resolving disagreements regarding money is a crucial element of creating a harmonious and happy relationship. Through identifying the differences in their attitudes toward money, establishing budgeting strategies and participating in long-term financial planning couples can cooperate in achieving their financial goals as well as build solid foundations for the future they will share.

Celebrating Differences

It's crucial to understand that the differences in attitude towards money could make a difference in relationships. If partners possess different points of view and strengths that complement one with their strengths and collaborate in order to accomplish common targets.

In this case, one of the partners might be more organised and focused with regards to budgeting, whereas another partner could be more inventive and innovative in figuring out ways to save money.

In celebrating the differences in these and acknowledging each other's strengths, the two partners will be able to build an even stronger and longer-lasting connection.

Respecting Boundaries

It's crucial to cooperate in managing financial matters, it's equally essential to recognize the boundaries of each other in relation to finances. It could mean making clear the boundaries of borrowing, spending as well as financial decision-making.

In this case, for instance, the partners could be able to agree to discuss their plans with one another prior to making major purchase or establish a maximum amounts of discretionary spending that the partners can each month.

It is also essential to protect the privacy of each other in the area of financial matters.

The partners should be careful not to snoop or trying to regulate the financial choices of their partners which could lead to anger and distrust.

Finding Common Ground

When tackling financial disagreements the most important thing is to focus in finding common ground, and pursuing common objectives. It could involve flexibility, compromise and inventive problem-solving.

If, for instance, one partner is more intent in saving money for the future, while another partner is more at ease in the present time, they might be able to come to an agreement by putting aside a particular amount of cash each month to fund savings but also permitting the possibility of spending some money on discretionary expenses.

Chapter 16: Handling Parents' Disagreements Parenting

One of the most enjoyable and difficult situations in the life of a person However, it is also a significant source of conflict within family relationships, especially if partners are different in their approach or opinions regarding the raising of children.

In this section we'll look at strategies to manage disagreements over parenting. These include ways to communicate, various parenting styles and ways of resolving issues regarding parenting styles.

Communication Strategies

Communication is crucial in settling disputes about parenting. The goal of parents is to speak openly, truthfully and with respect to their partners, even if they do not agree.

These are some strategies for communication to help parents deal with disagreements over parenting issues:

1. Active listening: The partners should be attentive to one another and attempt to comprehend the perspectives of each other. It involves asking questions, clearing up any confusion, and not making preconceived notions.

2. The ability to validate and empathize Partnerships should be approached by one others with understanding and acceptance and acknowledge that each person has different views and experiences. This will help to establish trust and understanding within the partnership.

3. "I-messages." Partners must utilize "I-messages" when expressing their opinions and worries instead of blame-shifting or praising the other. In other words instead of declaring "You always do this wrong," one of the partners could be able to say "I feel frustrated when this happens."

4. Time-outs: The partners should be taking breaks whenever necessary to avoid conflict

that escalates. This means taking a moment to step back in the dialogue and returning back when the feelings have subsided.

Different Parenting Styles

The parents may be different style based on their personal experiences, their cultural background or their personal beliefs. Common parenting styles are the permissive, authoritarian and assertive.

Parents who are authoritative are strict and imposing, and expect the same from their children. Parents who are permissive are more relaxed and accommodating as they allow their children the independence to decide for themselves. The parents who are assertive are nevertheless nurturing and help their children become autonomous and responsible.

If the parents of two people have different style of parenting, it may cause conflict and miscommunication. As an example, a strict parent might feel angry with the permissive spouse who permits children to violate rules. On the other hand, a permissive parent could be annoyed by an authoritative parent who is rigid and rigid.

Resolving Differences in Parenting Approach

To resolve disputes about parenting, parents must discover ways of resolving the differences in a positive and productive approach. It could involve negotiation, flexibility, compromise as well as creative solutions.

Below are a few suggestions to help parents come to an agreement on their how they parent:

1. Find common goals Partner should establish shared objectives and goals regarding the care of their children. This will allow them to focus on the things that matter most and collaborate towards common targets.

2. Flexible and cooperation: Both partners must be able to make compromises and remain open to change in the parenting style they choose to use. This could involve finding inventive solutions that are beneficial for both parents, like creating limits and expectations that align with the parenting style of both parents.

3. Get outside help: The partners could seek out external support from counsellors, family therapists or even a parenting consultant. They can offer guidance and help in resolving tensions and for building a stronger connection.

Here are a few examples of what is good practice for managing parenting disagreements:

1. Respect and Empathy Partner should treat one another in a manner that is respectful and compassionate acknowledging that all have different perspective and experiences.

2. Active listening: The partners should take the time to listen and attempt to comprehend their perspectives. This includes asking questions, debunking any confusion, and staying clear of the assumption that you know.

3. Flexible and compromising: Both partners are expected to accept compromise and flexibility on the way they handle their disagreements. It is possible to find creative solutions that are beneficial for both of them, like having goals and expectations that are shared that align with each other's parenting style.

4. Consistency: The partners should endeavor to remain consistent with their parenting style, particularly in regards to setting the boundaries and expectations of their children. This will help prevent the confusion that can arise between couples.

5. In search of outside assistance: Partners might want external support from

counsellors, family therapists or parenting consultant. They can offer guidance and help in resolving conflict and to build a stronger connection.

6. Dissolving conflict in a positive approach: The partners should try at resolving disputes in a positive way that includes active listening, empathy and compromise. It is important to avoid tactics that include blaming or criticizing or making threats or ultimatums.

7. Be mindful of the needs of the child Parents should be able to focus on their child's well-being and needs when it comes to addressing conflicts over parenting. It could mean putting aside personal disagreements as well as working in tandem towards achieving shared goals.

Parenting disagreements may be difficult, however using the correct communication methods or parenting methods, as well as ways to resolve conflicts, couples can build the foundation for a more positive and supportive relation. It's important to interact with the other person in a respectful and compassionate manner and also to be open and flexible when trying to find ways to work together for both parties. When you prioritize the needs of your child as well as their wellbeing, parents are able to create the foundation for a more healthy and harmonious family relationship.

Chapter 17: Dealing with Conflicts over Intimacy

Intimacy is a crucial aspect in any relationship that is romantic, however, disagreements over intimacy can be a challenge to handle. The reason for these disagreements is because of disagreements about sexual desire and expectations or even previous experiences. In this article we'll look at methods of communication, as well as understanding one of our needs and preferences, and ultimately methods of negotiation and compromise that can aid partners to resolve disagreements over sexual intimacy.

Techniques for Communication on Delicate Subjects

Intimate disagreements often touch on sensitive topics like sexual desire, preference as well as boundaries. It isn't easy to speak about these subjects freely and without being frightened or insecure. But, a clear and effective way of communicating is vital to solving those disputes.

1. Active listening practice: when talking about intimate subjects it's important to develop active listening. This means giving your companion the full attention of your time and striving to comprehend their viewpoint without interfering or getting defensive.

2. Make use of "I" statements: Using "I" statements can help you avoid blame or accusing your spouse. In other words instead of using the phrase "You never listen to my needs," think about using the phrase "I feel unheard when we don't talk about my needs."

3. Do not use labels or judgements Do not use judgements or labels when talking about sensitive issues. Instead, you should focus on writing about your personal experiences and feelings.

4. Schedule time to discuss topics Set aside a set period to have intimate discussions in order to make sure that each partner is well-prepared and focused. This will help avoid misunderstandings as well as distracting conversations.

Understanding Each Other's Needs

Being aware of each other's requirements is essential to resolving disputes about intimacy. The partners should be willing to consider the other's viewpoints and determine points where they might be in conflict.

1. Find out what each person needs Partner need to take the time to understand their wants and needs and also the needs and desires of their partners. This will help the two partners get to know each other's viewpoints and find the common ground.

2. Openly and truthfully The partners should speak openly and openly about their wants and wants, as well as taking care to respect

the boundaries of each other and their comfort level.

3. Accept compromises: The partners must be prepared to work together to satisfy each other's requirements. It could mean trying out different approaches or altering expectations.

4. Get outside help: Partner may wish to seek external help, like counseling or therapy, to aid them in understanding and deal with their personal disputes.

Compromise and Negotiation

Negotiation and compromise may assist partners to find solutions to the disagreements they have about intimacy. Here are some tips to assist partners in negotiating and negotiate effectively.

1. Set common goals: Partner must identify the common interests in relation to intimacy. It could be about building

confidence, improving pleasure or even exploring different experiences.

2. Prioritize your needs: Each partner ought to prioritize the wants and needs, while agreeing to make concessions on some issues.

3. Partner brainstorm solutions: The two parties must collaborate to come up with possible solutions to their differences. It could involve trying out different ideas, making new boundaries or seeking out outside help.

4. Ask for feedback: The partners should solicit feedback from one another during the negotiation process in order to make sure they're in the same boat.

5. Partner should be able and willing to alter their desires and expectations so that they can meet one another's requirements.

Example of Good Practice:

The couple of Emily and Michael have been struggling with intimacity issues. Emily is keen to try the new possibilities and experience different things. Michael prefers their existing routine. They agree to sit together and talk regarding their wants and needs.

Emily: "I really want to try new things in our intimacy, but I understand that it may be uncomfortable for you. Can we brainstorm some ideas and find a way to compromise?"

Michael: "I'm open to taking on new challenges, but I'm unsure how to begin. Could you provide me with some tips?

Chapter 18: Rebuilding Trust after an Argument

Everyone has conflicts and disagreements. it's normal for feelings to be high in these times. But, it's crucial that you know how to disagree with your spouse and not cause irreparable damages to the relationship. One of the biggest problems that can arise following an argument is to rebuild trust between your two partners. The chapter in this article will discuss the steps to rekindle trust following the conflict, which includes apologize and forgive, building trust, and then moving forward.

Apologizing and Forgiving

Reconciliation and forgiveness are vital actions to rebuild trust following disagreements. When we disagree with our spouse We may make comments or act in ways that hurt the other person, which could harm the relationship. An apology is an opportunity to admit the wrongdoing and accept the responsibility to our conduct. Sincere apology is based on understanding and willingness to apologize. An unsincere or sloppy apology is not enough to restore confidence.

In apologizing for something, it's important to provide specific details about your actions or the conduct that led to hurt. In other words the phrase "I'm sorry for everything" isn't enough to deal with the issue. Try to express yourself in a specific manner, such similar to "I'm sorry for the hurtful things I said during the argument." It shows you're responsible for your behavior and you are aware of the effect that they caused your spouse.

It is also essential to show apology with remorse. Recognizing remorse signifies acknowledging you recognize the harm and hurt that you have caused your spouse. This shows you are concerned about the feelings of your partner and you are determined to repair your relationship. Saying, for example "I feel terrible for what I said, and I understand how it hurt you" will help in creating confidence.

Forgiveness is the flip aspect of building confidence. To forgive is to let go of the hurt and anger that resulted from the dispute. The goal of forgiveness isn't to forget the events that occurred, but it's about acknowledging an apology, and then moving on. It's not always simple and it's essential to creating trust in relationships.

In the process of forgiveness, you need to make clear the actions or behavior you're granting forgiveness for. As an example, saying "I forgive you for the hurtful things you said during the argument" indicates that you're acknowledging your apology and moving on. You should also avoid the temptation of revisiting past mistakes, or harboring grudges. Forgiveness is about letting off the past and focus on the future and present.

Rebuilding Trust

Rebuilding trust after a dispute is a process that takes time and dedication. It's not something that could be accomplished in a single day and is crucial for an effective and long-lasting relationship. Building trust takes both parties to commit to fixing the harm caused by an disagreement.

One of the most important steps for regaining trust is communicating freely and truthfully. Both parties must openly discuss the issues and feelings they have with no fear of judgement or criticism. It is important to pay attention to the perspective of your partner and to be open to make compromises.

One way to restore trust is to develop an outline of the plans for the coming years. The plan must include steps or actions which both partners will be committed to. If, for instance, the disagreement was over one party not being able to communicate it could be a good idea to consist of a set amount of time every day for conversations with each others. This shows both parties are dedicated to making improvements in their relationship, and are prepared to take steps to reduce the likelihood of disputes.

To build trust, you must be constant with your behavior and actions. It's not enough just to make promises or apologize if you do not follow through on the promises. Being consistent shows you're committed to your relationship and committed to working hard to fix the harm caused by the disagreement.

Moving Forward

When you've apologized and forgiven and taken the necessary steps to building trust, it's time to continue moving forward. Moving forward is about getting rid of the past, and instead focus on the future and present. It is important not to dwell over the conflict and look at the positives of the relation.

Chapter 19: Seeking Professional Help

When it comes to relationships, conflict will always occur. Even the most affectionate and compatible spouses can experience conflicts and disputes. Although many couples have the ability to deal with these problems independently, others require assistance from professionals in navigating more complicated issues. A professional therapist may be helpful couples looking to understand how to disagree with each other without doing serious harm for their marriage.

Identifying the Need for Professional Help

A decision to seek out assistance from a professional isn't necessarily an straightforward one. Couples may be embarrassed or embarrassed when they admit they're having difficulties in their relationships. The truth is that seeking out professional assistance can be a sign of courage and not insecurity. This shows how the two are dedicated to improving their relationship, and will be willing to do what is necessary in the direction of improvement.

There are a variety of signs which indicate that you require assistance from a professional in the relationship. This includes:

1. Communication problems In the event that a couple are unable to communicate effectively, or if the communications have become negative or violent It could be the right the time to get professional assistance.

2. Conflicts that recur: If a couple fights time and time again with no resolution, or even making any progress, it could be a good idea to seek out expert help.

3. Intimacy loss: If you and your partner have lost that physical and emotional bond they used to have then it could be an appropriate time to consult a professional.

4. Life changes or trauma A couple may have suffered a traumatizing event that has

.y or the loss of a child or are an important life change for .e, a move or loss of employment or loss, it could be a good an appropriate time to seek out professional advice.

Finding a Qualified Therapist

Locating a therapist who is qualified can be difficult, however, it's crucial to choosing the best person for your relationship. It's crucial to locate someone who is specialized in couple therapy and is familiar with the particular issues that the couple are confronting. Here are some suggestions to find a therapist who is qualified:

1. Referrals: Contact your relatives, friends or a reputable medical professional for a recommendation. Anyone who has had positive results with therapy may be able to provide helpful information.

2. Find out about several therapists around the area and then read reviews of them. Search for therapists who are specialized in

therapy for couples and are familiar with working on the specific problems that the couple may be dealing with.

3. Initial consultation: Set up an initial appointment with a counselor to find out whether they're a suitable partner for each other. This will give couples to get questions answered and talk about their issues.

4. Credentials: Ensure that the therapist has been licensed with the proper certifications to perform therapy.

Committing to the Process

After the couple has located an expert counselor, it is crucial to take the time to commit to the procedure. Couples therapy is an emotional and challenging process However, it also can very fulfilling. Here are some suggestions for taking the plunge into therapy:

1. Honesty: Share your feelings to your therapist as well as to each other. Discuss

and feelings in a candid and ...ner.

...tive participation: Be active during ...erapy sessions. That means you're actively engaged with the therapy process and eager to experiment with new ideas.

3. Being open-minded: Open to fresh ideas and new perspectives. Therapy is a great way to challenge your assumptions and opinions, and it is important to open your mind to new ideas and ways to think.

4. The patience: Therapy isn't an instant fix. It takes patience and persistence for real improvement. Stay patient and determined to your goal.

To conclude, seeking expert help is a great alternative for couples looking to understand how to disagree with one another without creating serious harm in their relationships. Finding the need for help from a professional and finding a therapist who is qualified and agreeing to the process of therapy is a must on your journey towards a more healthy relation. Through the assistance of an experienced therapist as well as a determination to follow through, couples will be able to develop effective techniques for communicating, build trust, and improve the emotional bond. It is important to keep in mind the fact that seeking help from a professional isn't a sign of vulnerability, but instead it's a signal of confidence and willingness to improve the relationship.

Couples therapy also offer an open and secure place for couples to talk on difficult problems. An experienced therapist will aid the couple in identifying behaviors that could cause conflicts and offer techniques and methods to assist couples effectively communicate and control their emotional states.

It is important to remember that not every couple that seek help from a professional are able to salvage their marriage. Therapy

...provide the couple with the ...nd knowledge they require to ... with a positive attitude, regardless ...nether this means remaining with each ...ther or moving away.

Apart from the couples counseling Other resources are to couples experiencing difficulties. The resources available include books, internet-based resources as well as support groups. Couples should look at all the options available and figure out which one works for them.

A brief summary of seeking assistance from professionals is a great method for couples to understand how to communicate with one another without causing serious harm for their marriage. Finding the need for assistance from professionals and finding a therapist who is qualified and agreeing to the therapeutic process are crucial steps on the process.

www.ingramcontent.com/pod-product-compliance
Lightning Source LLC
Chambersburg PA
CBHW071442080526
44587CB00014B/1960